PENGUIN BOOKS

GET TO WORK

Linda R. Hirshman is retired from her position as the Allen/Berenson Distinguished Visiting Professor of Philosophy and Women's Studies at Brandeis University, where she taught courses on Western political philosophy and the regulation of sex and violence. She is the author of *Hard Bargains: The Politics of Sex* and *A Woman's Guide to Law School*. Hirshman also taught and practiced law in Chicago for many years, including trying three cases before the Supreme Court of the United States. She is married and has children.

Hirshman's article "Homeward Bound," on why women are trapped in the domestic world and how to get out, appeared in the December 2005 *The American Prospect*. She has appeared on *60 Minutes* and *Good Morning America,* speaking on the subject of women quitting their jobs to stay home. She is, proudly, number 77 in Bernard Goldberg's *100 People Who Are Screwing Up America.*

Visit www.gettoworkmanifesto.com

GET TO WORK

. . . And Get a Life, Before It's Too Late

LINDA R. HIRSHMAN

PENGUIN BOOKS

PENGUIN BOOKS

Published by the Penguin Group

Penguin Group (USA) Inc., 375 Hudson Street, New York, New York 10014, U.S.A.
Penguin Group (Canada), 90 Eglinton Avenue East, Suite 700, Toronto,
Ontario, Canada M4P 2Y3 (a division of Pearson Penguin Canada Inc.)
Penguin Books Ltd, 80 Strand, London WC2R 0RL, England
Penguin Ireland, 25 St Stephen's Green, Dublin 2, Ireland
(a division of Penguin Books Ltd)
Penguin Group (Australia), 250 Camberwell Road, Camberwell,
Victoria 3124, Australia (a division of Pearson Australia Group Pty Ltd)
Penguin Books India Pvt Ltd, 11 Community Centre,
Panchsheel Park, New Delhi – 110 017, India
Penguin Group (NZ), 67 Apollo Drive, Rosedale, North Shore 0745, Auckland,
New Zealand (a division of Pearson New Zealand Ltd)
Penguin Books (South Africa) (Pty) Ltd, 24 Sturdee Avenue,
Rosebank, Johannesburg 2196, South Africa

Penguin Books Ltd, Registered Offices:
80 Strand, London WC2R 0RL, England

First published in the United States of America by Viking Penguin,
a member of Penguin Group (USA) Inc. 2006
Published in Penguin Books 2007

1 3 5 7 9 10 8 6 4 2

Portions of this book first appeared as "Homeward Bound" in *The American Prospect*.

ISBN 0-670-03812-1 (hc.)
ISBN 978-0-14-303894-8 (pbk.)
CIP data available

Printed in the United States of America
Designed by Nancy Resnick

In memory of Betty Friedan
Author, in 1963, of *The Feminine Mystique*

GET TO WORK

HOMEWARD BOUND

I f Betty Friedan had lived just a little longer. We are about to restart the revolution. But now we have to do it without her.

For twenty-five years, she watched as the backlash generation slowly walked away from the promise of a better life. Women—whether they stay home or, like most women, just carry the responsibility for home to work and back—are homeward bound. Their men won't carry enough of the household to enable them to succeed fully in the public world. Glass ceiling? The thickest glass ceiling is at home.

Their bosses, who are mostly someone else's husband, won't do the job their own husbands turned down, so there is no employer day care, and there are precious few government tax breaks. Look deeply and you will see that liberal and conservative commentators largely agree that ideally women belong at home.

And women say they choose this fate, and the feminist movement backs them up.

"Choice feminism," the shadowy remnant of the original movement, tells women that their choices, everyone's choices, the incredibly constrained "choices" they made, are good choices. Everyone says if feminism failed it was because it was too radical. But we know—and surely the real radical, Betty Friedan, knew—that it wasn't because feminism was too radical. It was because feminism was not radical enough. A movement that stands for everything ultimately stands for nothing.

Bounding home is not good for women and it's not good for the society. The women aren't using their capacities fully; their so-called free choice makes them unfree dependents on their husbands. Whether they leave the workplace altogether or just cut back their commitment, their talent and education are lost from the public world to the private world of laundry and kissing boo-boos. The abandonment of the public world by women at the top means the ruling class is overwhelmingly male: If the rulers are male, they will make mistakes that benefit males. Picture an all-male Supreme Court. We may well go back there. What will that mean for the women of America?

Educated women opting out and working mothers throughout society doing 60 percent to 70 percent of the housework reveals a hard truth. Good economic research shows that women have squeezed as much out of their days as they can without more help. For all its achievements, feminism cannot make more progress, private or public, until it turns its spotlight on the family. Child care and housekeeping have satisfying moments but are not occupations likely to produce a flourishing life. Gender ideology places these tasks on women's backs; women must demand redistribution.

Happily, the solution is near to hand. As any philosopher, including this one, can tell you, the alternative to a meaningless "choice" is value, the value of a flourishing life. People have been discussing what it means to have a good life for thousands of years. The answer, in Western culture, always includes using your talents and capacities to the fullest and reaping the rewards of doing so. Friedan started this movement with such a "values feminism," when she described a good life in *The Feminine Mystique:* "Down through the ages man has known that he was set apart from other animals by his mind's power to have an idea, a vision, and shape the future to it . . . when he discovers and creates and shapes a future different from his past, he is a man, a human being."

At this moment, 55 percent of college undergraduates are female—girls who should have a vision and wish to shape the future to it, to aspire to something complex and demanding, which they know they can do well—become a great artist or a crusading prosecutor, own their own restaurant or start the next Starbucks, design the next wrap dress or the next iPod, be a lifesaving nurse, or the scientist who finds a cure for cancer. They may never get there, but however far they go—to the end of their abilities—the path is the path to a flourishing life. "Modern" society still puts roadblock after roadblock in their path. It will take a laser focus for women to reach their ambitions for a full human life. They must even resort to the love that dares not speak its name: love of work.

The world has changed since Friedan wrote, and now mere rhetoric—what we used to call consciousness raising—is not enough. It's a tough world. Women need a plan. Here's mine, for a start.

A STRATEGIC PLAN TO GET TO WORK

- Don't study art. Use your education to prepare for a lifetime of work.
- Never quit a job until you have another one. Take work seriously.
- Never know when you're out of milk. Bargain relentlessly for a just household.
- Consider a reproductive strike.
- Get the government you deserve. Stop electing governments that punish women's work.

I'll come back to the details later, but as this outline reflects, the changes that will bring women to the positions of power they deserve will come from many places. Change will start when women internalize centuries of hard-won insights into the content of a flourishing life. The next step is for women to stand up for themselves by making and keeping this plan or their own version of it, to lead a flourishing life. Men are not natural villains, but they will not make a fair deal on the home front unless women stand up and ask for one. As the economists say, they never met a man who washed a rented car before he returned it to the lot. It's an old story, but we'll tell it as long as we have to: Only when women make it necessary for men to take on a fair share of the family labor will they do so.

Starting the revolution at home does not rule out using the government. When I poked my head above the trench of choice feminism to suggest that moral categories apply to women's lives, I was immediately accused of trying to force women to abandon their homes and return to work. Stalinist! Nazi! Ultimately, Stalinists and Nazis can coerce only with the power of the state. I am not the state. But women are correct to feel they are being pushed. In the United States, the government interferes in women's lives all the time. All to push them back into the home. My favorite example is that the Internal Revenue Service taxes a married workingwoman's income much more heavily than a single woman's income. Just changing the tax law would do a lot to free up women to decide whether to return home or not.

If all of this sounds daunting, it's because for twenty-five years, the only messages women have heard are the ones telling them to forget their dreams and look homeward. For a generation, an acid rain of criticism has fallen daily on the heads of women trying to make a flourishing life in the larger world. No one would want to marry them, the mainstream media said; they were as likely to find a husband as be killed by a terrorist. They'd grow too old to have children, book writers warned them. If they had children, the poor things would be in the hands of "strangers." The only work available involves eighty-hour weeks. Stay-at-home moms suggest that only monsters of neglect would prefer adult work to children's play.

Once, workingwomen could seek refuge under the umbrella of economic need. But the newest move of the mommy bunch is to contend that mothers should never work unless the alternative is the direst poverty. This latest attack on working mothers is heavily, but stealthily, supported by the fundamentalist right. An innocent-looking guide to living without many material advantages, *So You Want to Be a Stay-at-Home Mom* by Cheryl Gochnauer turns out to be a New Testament sermon on the godliness of staying at home. Last year conservative commentator Danielle Crittenden told workingwomen that their lives were "just a pile of pay stubs."

About a year ago, a Washington, D.C., mom, Judith Warner, dared to question the tyranny of the new momism with her book, *Perfect Madness.* Her frank reportage was the first real critical look into the stifling home world they had created. But all she could recommend for a solution was the same old public day-care business that has gone nowhere since 1972. The family, to her, is an unsolvable "conundrum," not a place for equality. Books, magazines, blogs all are bursting with suggestions, like the one in a recent letter to the *Times,* that we "restructure the architecture of the work place." For what? To accommodate women in their role as caretaker of the patriarchal family? Why should the patriarchal workplace be bulldozed and the patriarchal family left untouched? It's perfect madness.

Don't get into the perfect madhouse to begin with, and if you're there, get out. Here's how.

THE WAY WE LIVE NOW

The Ultimate Bride, graduate of an Ivy League college and then an English acting school, with a most prestigious master's degree to boot, was the ideal subject for the *New York Times* featured Sunday wedding column "Vows." Walking down the aisle at her family farm, she wed her perfect counterpart, also master's-degree-bearing, and a rising star in the competitive world of global policy.

When she married, the ultimate bride was using her skills and training at a worthy nonprofit. Eight years later, when I tried to interview her for my book on marriage after feminism, I could not find her—or most of the other women who announced their weddings in the *New York Times* that month. He, on the other hand, Googled right up, on the Web site of his current employer, a consulting firm. I called him up.

"Where's your wife?"

"At home in Brooklyn taking care of our daughter."

So were the rest. Eighty-five percent of the thirty-plus January brides in the *New York Times* had left the workplace in whole or in part. All of them were highly educated—degrees in business, including MBAs, lawyers, journalists, an opera singer, doctors, master's of higher education. All of them had worked full time after graduation. Ninety percent of them had had babies since 1996. Half the mothers were not working at all. Roughly one third were in part-time work at varying distances from their education and training. And six of them were working full time.

Although calling women from the 1996 "Styles" section is hardly a scientific survey, the 2002 U.S. Census reports that only 46 percent of the women with graduate degrees and children under one work full time, 17 percent part time. Educated women with children up to eighteen are working 59 percent full time and 18 percent part time, increasing in numbers as the children age. On average, then, highly educated women with small children are working full time at about a fifty percent rate.

Perhaps more important, after three decades of increasing their workforce participation, the percentage of highly educated working mothers has stopped going up. The *New York Times'* part-time home and work columnist, Lisa Belkin, caused a great furor in 2003 when she "sampled" a group of the highly educated stay-at-home mothers she knew and proclaimed there was an "Opt-Out Revolution."

"Revolution" is probably overstating it, but something is clearly going on. In 2001, Harvard Business School professor Myra Hart surveyed the women of the classes of 1981, 1986, and 1991 and found that only 38 percent of female Harvard MBAs with children were working full time. A 2004 survey by the Center for Work-Life Policy of 2,443 women with a graduate degree or very prestigious bachelor's degree revealed that 43 percent of those women with children had taken at least a couple of years out, sometimes more than once, primarily for family reasons.

During the 1990s, I taught a philosophy course in sexual bargaining at a very good college. Each year, after the class reviewed the low financial rewards for child-care work, I asked how the students anticipated combining work with child rearing. At least half the female students described lives of part-time or home-based work. Guys expected their female partners to care for the children. (When I asked the young men how they reconciled that prospect with the manifest low regard the market has for child care, they were mystified. Turning to the women who had spoken before, they said, uniformly, "But she chose it.") Richard Posner, federal appeals court judge and occasional University of Chicago adjunct professor of law, reports that "everyone associated with [elite law schools] has long known . . . that a vastly higher percentage of female than of male students will drop out of the workforce to take care of their children."

If these women were sticking it out in the business, law, and academic worlds, now, thirty years after feminism started filling the selective schools with women, the elite workplaces should be proportionately female. They are not. Law schools have been graduating classes around 40 percent female for decades—decades during which both schools and firms experienced enormous growth. And although the legal population will be 40 percent female in 2010, in 2003, the major law firms had only 16 percent female partners, according to the American Bar Association. The Harvard Business School has produced classes around 30 percent female. Yet in 2002 only 15.7 percent of Wall Street's corporate officers are women, and a mere eight are Fortune 500 CEOs. The percentage of women in state legislatures has scarcely budged from 23 percent in 1997.

So what does this "elite minority" have to do with the rest of the world? These educated and privileged women matter. They matter because they are the most likely women to become the rising stars of the new economy—the future senators, deal makers, newspaper editors, research scientists, policy makers, television writers and movie producers, university presidents, and Supreme Court justices. Alarm bells should ring when people say things like elites don't matter only when the subject is women. You never see the *New York Times,* or for that matter the lefty *Nation* magazine, arguing that Congress's decisions don't matter, because most people aren't congressmen. Can you imagine the *Wall Street Journal* asserting that CEOs' decisions don't matter because most people can't aspire to be CEOs? Ever read in the sports page that quarterbacks don't matter because they are the elite of football teams? Or that Henry Ford IV doesn't matter because most auto workers are not presidents of Ford?

Why would leading *women* matter? Well, media surveys reveal, for instance, that if only one member of a television show's creative staff is female, the percentage of women on-screen goes up from 36 percent to 42 percent. A world of 84 percent male lawyers and 84 percent female assistants is a different place from one with women role models in positions of social authority. Think of a big American city with an 84 percent white police force. If role models don't matter, consider how an all-male Supreme Court is going to feel. We are about to find out, I fear. Highly educated women's abandonment of the workplace is not an extension of the centuries of upper-class arm candy; it's a sex-specific brain drain from the future rulers of our society.

But interestingly these select women are not alone. Without regard to class, in 2004, only 38 percent of married mothers with husbands and children under one in the house worked full time—13 percent work part time, another 3 percent are looking for work. Married women with children under five and a husband around worked at a rate of only 62 percent, but,

again, about one third of that statistic is probably women doing part-time work. Whether the trend is for increasing participation or not, the raw numbers are low. Moreover, the
assignment of responsibility for the household to women applies in every social class.

Quite by chance the mommy blogosphere produced addi-
tional anecdotal evidence of how broad the homeward bound
phenomenon is. In response to my recent article on the subject, BloggingBaby.com (a Web site that advertises and dis-
cusses baby care, baby products, maternity clothes, etc.)
solicited stories of stay-at-home moms, apparently thinking
their reports would rebut my work. The BloggingBaby.com
mothers do not for the most part appear to be the same so-
cioeconomic class that the *Times* brides are, so the seven pro-
files published in December and January make a little picture
of how regular people behave. Surprise! The statistics are identical: Three of the seven moms don't work at all, three have
part-time jobs at increasing distances from their education and
training, and one works full time at what she was educated for.

Two of the three full-time moms never finished their educations. Ammie, profiled January 10, 2006, is "a thesis short of
[her] Masters in Applied History." Christine, January 4, 2006,
"was thinking I would go to grad school. . . . When I graduated, I had burned out on school and went into the work force
as an entry-level computer programmer." While Michelle, December 21, 2005, successfully completed law school, she "never
really thought much about money," winding up "100,000
[dollars] in debt" and therefore unable to work at the practice
she had envisioned. Although they didn't have such great op-

portunities as the *Times* brides, they also failed to find satisfying work, often before childbirth.

Like the *Times* brides, these women are completely dependent upon their husbands. Ammie's husband's "income is our sole source of support." Christine's "husband's income is just slightly less than our combined incomes were when we met. When we first met, he was making slightly more than I was, but his income grew much quicker than mine did from there." Deeply in debt, Michelle was not able to resist pressure from her husband to leave New York and move to his home state of Oregon.

Strapped as the families are, like the *Times* brides, they have no plans ever to return to work. After "working out of her home part time, making her own hours, and not having to answer to someone looking over her shoulder constantly," Ammie "cannot and will not do it again." Christine doesn't "ever want to work in the corporate world again." She knows she doesn't "have the stomach for the politics and stress that go along with an executive position." Michelle failed the Oregon bar and plans to skip the next two exam dates. She is "unwilling to work 70–90 hours a week just to make some corporation richer at the expense of my family."

With both groups, it's hard to know which came first—the failure in the education and alienation from the workplace or the reshuffled priorities of children and family. Unlike the richer women I studied, however, the cost of child care also played a role in the blogging mommies' decision. Even Ammie says she quit in part because "we were spending more money on child care than it was worth for me to work at that 'regular' job anyway." Christine was "stuck in a job that [she] didn't really like. . . . It got depressing to be working just to pay the nanny and fill up my 401k." Michelle says that "while all this was going on . . . I began to fall in love with my children. I began to love my husband more." Yet she, too, admits that her decision is partly driven by economics. "If I work at a smaller firm, I still have to put in 50 or 60 hours a week, occasional nights and weekends, and my salary will once again be eaten up by child-care." (This is obviously absurd: A lawyer in private practice working fifty hours a week makes more than any nanny except Mary Poppins.) Socially privileged women and just regular folks. Highly educated and the whole American female workforce. All the data reflect that women are tied to the household today in a way that rebuts every expectation of the feminist movement.

The reports are almost always couched in a description of the family that sounds eerily like a religious experience. Consider the endlessly repeated canard I never met a man who wished on his deathbed he had spent more time at work. What does this really mean? It's manifestly false—think Mozart. It devalues the world of work—and other public service—and elevates the world of the family to the experience closest to the afterlife.

If the nuclear family is the path to heaven, most of humanity must be somewhere else. Any good history of the family reports that work was separated from home only recently, in the industrialized West, maybe a century and a half ago. Before that, everyone in almost every family on earth worked. The placement of the nuclear family at the center of the moral universe and the assignment of child rearing exclusively to women is no more than two hundred years old. Indeed, most emotional ties were much broader, even to 1900: People cared equally for their extended families, the brotherhood of lodges, and even their mistresses.

The flip side of the caregiving women are the grateful men. These are the guys, beavering away at their high-status, high-paying, dangerous, interesting, courageous, political, public lives, who write me and anyone else who asks about how grateful they are to have such wonderful wives to raise the couples' children. "I thank God every day that my wife stays home with the kids. It makes my job, here and overseas, a lot easier to do knowing they are safe." Arguing that I am un-Christian, the president of the Southern Baptist Theological Seminary admits that he "respond[s] to Hirshman's arguments from a highly privileged position—as the son, husband, and son-in-law of women who gave and give themselves to the calling of motherhood without reservation."

The new, hyperdomesticated family reflects the convergence of two modern trends, one from the left and one from the right. On the left, people complaining about the supposed burden of labor in the market economy. The blogosphere and the correspondence columns in newspapers and magazines are full of letters from people who hate their jobs. "The workplace is nothing to get excited about: The majority of jobs outside the home are repetitious and socially invisible, and many of those jobs (men's especially) are physical as well . . . while prestige careers in law and business demand a degree of intensity and one-way commitment (employee to company, never vice versa) that would unbalance anyone's life, if one isn't unbalanced already." Perhaps the current generation, raised to believe there were no limits on their talents, experienced the realities of the workplace as an unusually nasty shock.

But just because work isn't as wonderful as people fantasized does not mean it isn't usually the best alternative available. *Perfect Madness* gives us an unforgettable look at the downside of domesticity. The women "had surrendered their better selves—and their sanity—to motherhood . . . pulled all-nighters hand-painting paper plates for a class party . . . obsessed over the most minute details of playground politics. . . . They dressed in kids' clothes—overall shorts and go-anywhere sandals. They ate kids' foods. They were so depleted by the affection and care they lavished upon their small children that they had no energy left, not just for sex, but for feeling like a sexual being."

The conservative side says that it is okay to withdraw from the rest of society to the selfish precincts of the family. This trend is perfectly captured by the postings on BloggingBaby.com from women who cannot imagine anything more important than the claims of their "own" children. One such mom wrote me recently: "After my first child was born I realized that I would soon be faced with sending my children to school. Public school is not for my family. Private school can not be afforded on my husband's salary. So I have chosen to homeschool. Now I feel that my 'giving back to society,' my 'mark on the world,' is my choice . . . to homeschool our children." So instead of trying to fix the public schools or the public policies that produce schools that are (for unidentified reasons) "not for MY family," all of the education and investment in this woman will now be directed only to her two children and no one else.

Of course, there are arguments against both trends: Working in the market economy has many rewards—of power, honor, money, exercise of capacities, and so on. And people ought to care about someone who isn't related to them by blood or marriage. But even if men and women hate working in the market economy and men and women don't give a darn about their public schools, that still leaves the question: Why is it that it's always the women—not the men—who wind up doing most of the work at home? Since people still have to eat, it almost without exception means men are taking off for work and leaving the women . . . homeward bound.

CHOOSING YOUR CHOICE

The most disheartening part about women's deciding to stay home is that they say doing so is their choice. "Choice" is the weasel word, and it is legitimated, especially for women who consider themselves liberals, because it's been adopted by the feminist movement. Even the most empowered women do not see how narrow their options are at the moment of "choice."

A couple of years ago, I was on *60 Minutes* with a woman who had been the editor of the *Stanford Law Review* and was working, by all accounts successfully, at a huge and prestigious New York law firm. Not yet thirty, married to a would-be surgeon, she had a baby in the second year of her career, just as he started his surgical residency. With a straight face, she told the camera that "someone had to take care of the baby, and it certainly wasn't going to be a surgical resident." Since she only likes to do things perfectly, she felt she could not juggle two roles, so she "chose" to quit and has been unemployed for al-most a decade. There was no discussion at all of her other, ear-lier, choices: her choice to marry an aspiring surgeon who felt he could not take care of the baby; her choice to have a baby at the beginning of his surgical residency, when he was least able to help out; her choice of indulging her perfectionism, condemning her to spend her talents on tasks that people with no degree at all can do, in which she would never be judged, wanting or no, a kind of miniaturist in the business of life. Had she not made all these other choices, when the baby ar-rived, she might have actually had more choice about what would happen to her career.

No one wants to face it. Stay-at-home moms do not like to hear that the sacrifice of their education, talents, and prospects to their spouses' aspirations and their children's needs was a mistake, so they contend the stay-at-home decision cannot be judged. "It was my choice." End of discussion. On the other side, workingwomen are glad to use the right to choose to pro-tect themselves from the chorus of voices from the right telling them to go home. The epitome of the choice strategy had to be when *Sex and the City*'s Charlotte tried to justify to her lawyer friend, Miranda, her decision to quit her job in part in response to pressure from her insufferable first husband. "I choose my choice!" Charlotte intoned repeatedly. "I choose my choice!"

Both the stay-at-home and working moms often consider themselves feminists. They reasonably make this claim be-cause feminism has actively encouraged women to run from a fight by embracing any decision a woman makes as a feminist act. I have dubbed this watered-down version of feminism choice feminism.

The dynamic started in the very early years of the feminist movement. Originally, feminism was defined by the campaign for rights and opportunities, because women had very few of either, and very few choices. The result of that first wave of feminism was choice, and Friedan was the trumpeter, calling women to choose something different for themselves. Friedan was pretty clear on what the right choice was—she likened housework to the labor of an animal, and she wasn't much interested in an endless spiral of more and more worthy causes for feminism to include in its embrace.

Part of that choice became the long feminist battle over who should justly exercise the legal power to determine women's reproductive fates. The *Oxford English Dictionary* lists the usage of "pro-choice" at least as early as 1975, a mere two years after the Supreme Court decision in *Roe v. Wade.* But my first sighting of the language of choice is earlier and more meaningful than that. In some long-forgotten time, abortion advocates actually thought they could mobilize substantial support for legal abortion from the liberal elements in the Catholic Church; the 1972 organization was called Catholics for a Free Choice. Whoever found it first, the point is that saying "choice" was initially a way not to have to say "abortion."

In those decades, women were finding ways to choose paths that increased their power and their status in society. But the feminist movement couldn't hold on to this important goal—and this was its critical failure. Instead, the movement came to define choice as an umbrella to put over anything any

woman said she had decided to do. In large part, this happened because Gloria Steinem was too gracious for our own
good. Just over thirty years ago, the feminist movement turned
from Betty Friedan, the big-nosed, razor-tongued moralist to
the beautiful, ever-gracious, and all-inclusive Gloria Steinem.
It seemed a natural decision at the time, but the effects have
been ruinous.

There's a wonderful story about it in Judith Hennessee's bi-
ography of Betty Friedan. "In 1972, Kingman Brewster, then
president of Yale, told an audience of graduate women that he
could accept the part of the movement represented by Gloria
[Steinem]—the part that included men," but not the supposedly
man-hating philosophy of Friedan. Brewster had it completely
backward. Married and the mother of three, Betty Friedan focused her entire energy on the problem of work and family life
for the middle-class American woman. Single throughout the
feminist heyday and childless to the end, Gloria Steinem ruled
the movement when one of its theme songs was "a woman needs
a man like a fish needs a bicycle."

Still, Brewster was right about one thing: Gloria was nicer
than Betty. If anyone was suited to steer a radical and judgmental movement into useless choice feminism, it was the
confrontation-averse Gloria Steinem. Under her uncritically
accepting eye, feminism expanded to embrace every oppressed
group. Steinem's biographer, Sydney Ladensohn Stern, put her
finger on the difference: "Betty . . . is a big thinker. I didn't think
of Gloria in the same league. She's a good consensus builder, but
was defending an ideologically narrower viewpoint—political
correctness—and she seemed insecure about how much she was

willing to stand up and say what she really stood for . . . she was a careful operator." Salon.com's Laura Miller shares the telling story that a college friend once dragged the strangely passive activist by the leg down a hallway, shouting, "Why don't you ever get angry? Get angry!"

Part of this failure was personality. But partly it was also because feminists were stared down by women on the other side. Almost from the beginning, antifeminists, like the opponents of the Equal Rights Amendment, organized by Phyllis Schlafly, claimed that feminism wanted to control peoples' personal lives. (Would that they were right!) Schlafly charged that passage of the ERA would lead to men's abandoning their families, unisex toilets, gay marriages, and women in the army. All of this has now happened, with no sign of the world's ending yet, yet Schlafly succeeded beyond her wildest imaginings.

Schlafly's domesticity was never some bliss of choice; she advocated a religiously dictated, sex-driven dependency. It was 1976, when Indiana was on the verge of becoming the thirty-fifth state to ratify the ERA, when Schlafly says she realized she needed to seek support from the churches. For her vision, she says she got "1,000 mainline Protestants, evangelicals, Catholics, Mormons and orthodox Jews" to attend an anti-ERA rally in Springfield, Illinois. "That is when the pro-family movement was invented," she says. "It was a coming together of believers of all denominations who would do two things—come into politics for the first time and then work together for a cause they shared."

Instead of challenging the legitimacy of orthodox religion as a source for public policy, feminism made the fatal error of denying the charges: We're not feminazis and we don't want to tell you how to live your life. We only want to give you opportunities. Whether individual women take their places in the public world is up to them. It's their choice.

So while Steinem was giving cocktail parties in the Hamptons for Cesar Chavez, and Schlafly was putting the tradition in traditional family, feminists retreated to the arena they could defend—that the public world should be open to women who wanted to work there. Building on the innocuous prohibition of employment discrimination based on sex, in the race-oriented 1964 Civil Rights Act, conventional women like Ruth Bader Ginsburg at the ACLU began a legalistic, culturally circumspect campaign to open the office doors to women.

In the drive to offend no one, the feminist movement abandoned the home front. The radical Friedan didn't turn her attention to the family until 1981, in *The Second Stage,* and by then she had lost her edge. The tone of the book is dispirited and full of useless, grandiose, and wishful rhetoric ("women and men even now are transcending sex-role polarization . . . we can transcend that false antagonism between feminism and the family . . . and move beyond sexual politics"). All that transcendence was unworthy of the sixties radical she had once been, and the book was ignored. Real change occurred in the public world. But between the politically correct antipatriarchal singles like Steinem and the carefully bowtied Justice Ginsburg, the family slipped away, untouched by the corrosive principles of feminism.

The result of this was the preservation of the most intransigent of patriarchal institutions in our society. And that's where the trouble lay. Feminism did not lack the resources to recognize the problem. Very radical early writing included Pat Mainardi's political analysis of housework, which is riveting to this day. "Here's my list of dirty chores: buying groceries, carting them home and putting them away; cooking meals and washing dishes and pots; doing the laundry; digging out the place when things get out of control; washing floors. The list could go on but the sheer necessities are bad enough. All of us have to do these things, or get someone else to do them for us. The longer my husband contemplated these chores, the more repulsed he became, and so proceeded the change from the normally sweet, considerate Dr. Jekyll into the crafty Mr. Hyde who would stop at nothing to avoid the horrors of housework. As he felt himself backed into a corner laden with dirty dishes, brooms, mops and reeking garbage, his front teeth grew longer and pointier, his fingernails haggled and his eyes grew wild. Housework trivial? Not on your life! Just try to share the burden."

Instead, institutional feminism adopted a set of formal policies about housework. The National Organization for Women recommended "provision of independent Social Security coverage, including disability, in the homemaker's own name, portable in and out of marriage, and continuing as the homemaker leaves and re-enters the paid workforce" and demanded that unpaid caregiving be included in the calculation of the gross domestic product. Such policies, however, never took on the core problem—the conventional assignment of the household to women. Even in 2006, NOW's "family" initiative is all about building caring coalitions and funding child care and family leave in the public sphere rather than taking on the inequality where it lives.

The final step toward choice feminism came as women got to the workplace in large numbers in the 1970s and 1980s and then found themselves doing everything. It turned out they would be allowed to go to work, but at the same time they wouldn't be allowed out of the home. And instead of asking Why do I have to do it all in order to have it all? they decided they really didn't have to have it all, cut their ambitions off at the knees, and reverted to choice. Instead of thinking their way out of the dilemma to the path of status and power, they simply appropriated the language of choice from the liberating choices the movement started. Thus, although it was really a backlash, the language of choice anointed any decision at all about what life path to follow.

The leveling off of women's professional ambitions today shows us one truth: Without a movement to support them, women are not choosing the path to status and power alone. My little survey of the brides of the *Times* reflects that feminism lost even the women who had the most opportunity to *choose* the path toward status and power—the geeky and quirky intellectuals, not the prom queens and debutantes. Take a look at any Sunday *Times*. Although most of the brides have the bloom of youth, the wedding portion of the "Styles" section no longer resembles a debutante party. Just to cite a random example, on Sunday, January 15, 2006, the featured "Vows" bride, a Ph.D. from Cambridge University, was the curator of manuscripts at the Folger Shakespeare Library in Washington. Other brides included a medical student who was magna cum laude at Harvard; a Harvard Law grad associate at Arnold & Porter; an ob-gyn, cum laude from Columbia; deputy director in the Mayor's Office of Special Projects and Community Events in New York with a master's degree in public administration from Columbia; and so on.

I don't know them personally, but I can bet they were the ones who read *Pride and Prejudice* and identified with Elizabeth, the sharp-tongued and clever daughter of modest means who captured Darcy with her high-spirited independence, not the pale, mute daughter Lady Catherine de Bourgh had in mind for him. These were the girls who were going to make their lives from their wits and their brains, not their looks, trust funds, and reproductive organs. Immensely desirable mates, they should have been able to find spouses whose needs would not require, overtly or covertly, that they quit their jobs. Gifted with capacities for refined scholarship, human healing, legal reasoning, and educated to use the capacities, they were the women for whom the constraints of the feminine mystique were the most unjust. The twentieth-century feminist movement was the beginning, opening up the public world of work to women but leaving the family untouched. The Opt-Out Revolution may be in reality only a leveling off, but in this context it is the end of the beginning.

Deafened by choice, here's the moral analysis these women never heard: The family—with its repetitious, socially invisible, physical tasks—is a necessary part of life and has obvious emotional and immediate rewards, but it allows fewer opportunities for full human flourishing than public spheres like the market or the government. This less flourishing sphere is not the natural or moral responsibility only of women. Therefore, assigning it to women is unjust. Women assigning it to themselves is equally unjust.

The choice is a false one, based on the realities of a half-revolutionized society. Once we recognize that, we can admit that the tools feminism offered women to escape the dilemma have failed. This book is an effort to try a different approach. It is time for a new radicalism. Fortunately, the roots are sound.

WE'VE BEEN SPEAKING MORALITY ALL ALONG

One of BloggingBaby.com's profiled women blogged recently, "It's not my duty or any other woman's duty to advance the social and working status of women everywhere. I think we have reached a point . . . that we can be a bit more focused on our own personal choices and if we wish to focus on our families than [sic] that is our own damn business." In the mind of this writer, there could be no moral connection between her individual decision and the opinions of teachers like Posner or, worse, employers, regarding the prospects for their female students or employees. She may or may not be right that other women's well-being shouldn't outweigh the well-being of her children. But "our own damn business" silences the discussion of her decision completely.

Not only is she making a bad argument—her decision to focus on her family *will* have a social impact—but she's trying to hide the social harm she will do by putting it in a place where no one can look at it by using the magic language "choices" and "own damn business."

The problem with this argument is that "choice," or even its pumped-up cousin "personal choice," does not remove decisions to a special realm where they cannot be judged. As Mark Twain said, "A man who chooses not to read is just as ignorant as a man who cannot read." A woman who decides staying home with her children matters more than the fate of other women ought to be prepared to defend that position. Like the argument that elites don't matter if they're female, the position that women's choices are unworthy of moral analysis raises the ugly possibility that women's choices don't matter because women don't matter. Finally, refusing to analyze the decision only deludes women into thinking that they are choosing from a complete set of options, when there's a powerful social system in place directing them homeward.

This is a huge loss. First, there is no such thing as a morality-free life. Whether seeking religious salvation or secular honor or more toys, everyone tries to direct their lives to what seems to them to be good. So saying it's "our own damn business" doesn't really mean that the woman is making life decisions at random, throwing darts at a board that says WORK in one square, HOME in another, SELL YOUR ORGANS FOR MONEY in a third, and BECOME A WHORE in the fourth. She's making a moral analysis. She just doesn't want to have to defend it.

As we saw from our glimpse of the censure heaped on working mothers for all these backlash years ("a pile of pay stubs," remember?), people never stopped judging. It's just that the stay-at-home moms grabbed the moral high ground and now they want to pull the ladder up and stop the discussion. I am not going to play that game. When feminism returns to an analysis of the value of the choices women make, it will have the advantage of doing what everyone is doing all along, every time they enter a voting booth, every time they gossip, and every time they decide a legal case: making moral decisions about their lives and the lives of their society.

Most of the women I interviewed actually revealed a covert, but long-standing life plan to quit work and devote themselves to future husbands and children, regardless of the dependency and other issues that were waiting. People hate to confront that fact. When the *New York Times* ran an article about how girls at prestigious Yale College were planning their MRS degrees, the Internet went ballistic and pressed the *Times* to say its reporter was mistaken. Although the paper "explained" a little on their Web site, the actual Yale girls interviewed never really said they were misquoted. When pressed later, they just said they were deciding only for themselves. Own damn business.

The most obvious example of people making moral decisions for one another is, of course, voting. Many of the women on BloggingBaby.com are from Oregon. When the none-of-your-damn-business women voted in the Oregon referendum on the right to die (Oregon is the only state with a right to seek physician-assisted suicide), they were voting their morality on the rest of society. Presumably they voted for the right to die because they thought physician-assisted suicide was a good thing for people in desperate end-of-life situations and not because they thought it was murder but also none of their damn business. Or vice versa. Similarly, voting for higher taxes is a judgment that money will do more good redistributed around the community, to alleviate poverty or educate children, say, than it will in the hands of the individual who worked for it. Voting for lower taxes is a judgment that the money will do more good in the hands of the individual who worked for it than redistributed around the community.

We all, including liberals, make moral judgments every day. But somehow conservatives get all the moral ink. The conservative moral position is that women should stay home and keep house and raise the children. In his book on the subject, *It Takes a Family,* Republican Pennsylvania senator, Rick Santorum, lays it out: "What happened in America so that mothers and fathers who leave their children in the care of someone else—or worse yet, home alone after school between three and six in the afternoon—find themselves more affirmed by society? Here, we can thank the influence of radical feminism. . . . Sadly," the professional politician and U.S. senator Santorum continues, "the radical feminists succeeded in undermining the traditional family and convincing women that professional accomplishments are the key to happiness."

The conservative position, often linked to a resurgent religious fundamentalism, is so embedded in the culture that it has become invisible. When a commentator on the conservative Institute for American Values Web site asked "why Linda Hirshman considers it any of her freakin' business how I live my life," another institute member pointed out that "the entire purpose of the Institute whose board you're commenting on is to make it their business how other people live their lives." Whereupon the American Values board member replied, "Boy, they had me fooled. I thought their purpose was to strengthen the family. A pretty important cause considering the family is the foundation on which our society is built." Not telling people how to live their lives; just the old natural and invisible value-neutral foundational family. Who cannot love that? No wonder even some of the childless members of the conservative Independent Women's Forum call these ideologists of mandatory motherhood like Danielle Crittenden "mommy Nazis."

After decades of hearing women's work described as a "pile of pay stubs," working mothers mostly just want the debate to stop. Political conservatives, who have been moralizing all along, love this lowering of the curtain of moral silence over feminist claims. Libertarians believe that nothing happens on any level but the individual level. Social conservatives love it because they believe women belong at home, and working mothers' moral silence completely disempowers women from trying to act together to make a different large social structure. Finally, men with stay-at-home wives, liberal or conservative, love it since it disempowers women from acting singly in their unjust households, because they have no tools to identify the injustice that put them in the position of having to choose half a life either way.

It's time to reintroduce moral analysis into the discussion. When feminism stands up for flourishing lives for women, rather than just "choices," the get-yourself-home gang, especially on the right, can't just engage in name calling, like Santorum and Crittenden do. They have to defend *their* prescription for women, and when they do, they say really dumb things. They say women have flourishing lives in the home, because women are natural domestics, like naturally domestic female monkeys in the monkey world or naturally domestic prehistoric women were in the Stone Age. They say, as nationally syndicated columnist David Brooks said, from his office high above Times Square, that the hand that rocks the cradle rules the world. When opponents say dumb things, women have a chance.

If women take a lesson, they will learn that using their capacities for speech and reason, engaging in political life with other adults, having social and economic independence, and giving more to the society than they take cannot be reduced to a "pile of pay stubs." Never met someone dying who wished they'd had more time at work? Eleanor Roosevelt, Sojourner Truth, Elizabeth Cady Stanton, Jane Austen, Elizabeth I, Wolfgang Amadeus Mozart, Howell Raines, Franz Schubert, Martin Luther King, Jr., Karl Rove, Albert Einstein, Pablo Picasso, Abraham Lincoln, Bill Clinton, John XXIII, your candidate here. Betty Friedan said it and feminism just needs to touch that stone again.

FEMINISM COULD USE A FEW DEAD WHITE MEN

Who does Linda Hirshman think she is, that she can tell us how to lead our lives? Don't study art? Don't pick up the trash?

Don't have two children? In many circles "who do you think you are" is regarded as a knock-down argument, protecting the speaker from ever examining their life. There is an easy answer to how I can suggest better lives. Like Isaac Newton said, "If I have seen further . . . it is by standing upon the shoulders of Giants."

They were first spotted walking along the roadway to Athens from the port nearby.

"When we had finished our prayers and viewed the spectacle, we turned in the direction of the city; and at that instant Polemarchus the son of Cephalus chanced to catch sight of us from a distance as we were starting on our way home, and told his servant to run and bid us wait for him." (Plato, *The Republic,* Book I.)

They waited. By the end of the trip to and from the port of Athens, the longest dialogue in Western history was begun: What is the content of a good life? Whether we are aware of it or not, whether we like it or not, we live in a world that the dialogue created. If we are Christians, we are the heirs of Plato, through the philosopher-saint Augustine. If we are liberal Democrats, Plato started it with his call to imagine a good city. If we are Fascists, blame Plato's guardian state. All social movements, including feminism, at its roots, ultimately rest on a concept of a good life. Otherwise, why bother?

The ancient Greeks, like Plato and his student Aristotle, didn't have much to start with, so they began by asking what people are like and how people are different from animals, our closest relatives. A good life for humans would be different from a good life for horses. We differ, they observed, because we have speech and reason in addition to emotions and animal appetites like hunger, and because we live in organized groups.

A good life, they concluded, would therefore include exercising the capacities that are uniquely human and those that enable people to live in groups. Those would be politics and philosophy, and enlightened people would display courage, piety, generosity, and prudence. In a good society, people would rule and be ruled in turn so they could use their capacities both to be good governors and good citizens. Later thinkers added the value of freedom to make moral decisions, and, finally, the third standard of doing more good than harm.

I am not the first to apply the long-standing insights of philosophy to women's lives. Forty years ago, in *The Feminine Mystique,* Betty Friedan said, "[V]acuuming the living room floor—with or without makeup—is not work that takes enough thought or energy to challenge any woman's full capacity. . . . Down through the ages man has known that he was set apart from other animals by his mind's power to have an idea, a vision, and shape the future to it . . . when he discovers and creates and shapes a future different from his past, he is a man, a human being."

Taking the first standard first, women undoubtedly have capacities for speech and reason. Just to take the *Times* brides as an example, they showed their great capacities at every step along their very competitive educations. Many of them had succeeded in various human institutions—work, volunteer work, ordinary social life—demonstrating the political virtues of courage and prudence. Picking a random instance, for example, the med student from January 15 was an officer of The Creative Center, an organization helping people who have to live with cancer. Succeeding at politics with a small "p," including the politics of the workplace, takes prudence, discipline, and a gift for rhetoric.

By any measure, a life of housework and child care does not meet these standards for a good human life. The *Family Issues Encyclopedia* reports that women do the least pleasant tasks, most of which are relentless, obligatory, and performed in isolation. The lonely and never-ending aspects of women's housework contribute to increased depression for U.S. housewives. And here's what it feels like to Michigan working mother Joan Cummins. "It's the everyday things that get under your skin." When she arrived home one recent day from her job as a bank vice president, she found a dishwasher full of clean dishes needing to be put away and used cups by the sink. "How come you didn't empty the dishwasher?" she asked her husband, who arrives home earlier from his job as an insurance agent. The *New York Times* recently ran an article about a group of mothers of infants who, following a new movement to eliminate diapers, spend all their time watching their diaperless children for signs of elimination.

These are easy examples. But consider the values in a letter I received recently. The writer prefaced the letter by announcing that she was a Harvard graduate, and then described her life as a stay-at-home mom: "I dance and sing and play the guitar and listen to NPR. I write letters to my family, my congressional representatives, and to newspaper editors. My kids and I play tag and catch, we paint, we explore, we climb trees and plant gardens together. We bike instead of using the car. We read, we talk, we laugh. Life is good. I never dust."

Assuming she is telling the truth, and she does live in the perfect land of a Walgreens' ad, is not all this biking and tree climbing a bit too much of the inner child for any normal adult? Although child rearing, unlike housework, is important and can be difficult, it does not take well-developed political skills to rule over creatures smaller than you are, weaker than you are, and completely dependent upon you for survival or thriving. Certainly, it's not using your reason to do repetitive, physical tasks, whether it's cleaning or driving the car pool. My correspondent's life does have a certain Tom Sawyerish quality to it, but she has no power in the world. Why would the congressmen she writes to listen to someone whose life so resembles that of a toddler's, Harvard degree or no?

Since the Enlightenment, philosophers have expressed the second big standard for a good life—no one should be a slave to another man, even to a king. People are born free, they have proclaimed for centuries, and are endowed with inalienable rights to life, liberty, and the pursuit of happiness. Only a free will can achieve true moral meaning, the German philosopher Immanuel Kant added later. This philosophy seems tailor-made for choice feminism, right? Because we respect freedom we respect women's rights to choose any life they see fit.

But what happens when they choose a life that takes away their ability to make any further independent choices? Then choice bites its own tail. The women of the *Times*—and the more than 50 percent of all women the census says are not working full time—are not independent anymore. They are dependent on the productivity and continuing goodwill of the men they married. They cannot support themselves or their children. They cannot decide where the family is going to live. This lesson surfaced in the most graphic way in the *New York Times* on the first day of this year, 2006, in the form of an essay by Terry Martin Hekker, who had had her fifteen minutes of fame years ago as the author of a book advising women to ignore feminism and stay home with their husbands. On her fortieth anniversary, he gave her paper—divorce paper. One year later she was eligible for food stamps.

Although this is an extreme story, it is not an aberration. We cannot see into everyone's bedroom, but we have data about who wields the power in the male-earner family. Not only is there a wealth of economic studies of how power in the outside world translates into the family, but every stay-at-home mom I interviewed from the *Times* announcements was living in the town where her husband's work took him. The blogs are full of women, like Miriam Peskowitz, the author of *The Truth Behind the Mommy Wars,* who described her separation from her tenure track job as follows: "I worked as a professor until my daughter was born. . . . My university was an eight-hour drive from where my husband and I lived." At no point does this women's studies major and author of a book on work/family conflict mention what in the world she was doing eight hours from her job. Other online data reveal that her home was where her husband lived, but the interviewer never even asked her. In the world of mommy blogs the woman locating at the place where the man works, regardless of the price for her own aspirations, is so common that it appears to be a law of nature. It's not. It's the result of the unspoken bargain with the guy who provides the health insurance.

Finally, even people mostly unaware of the centuries-long discussion of a good life know that you are supposed to try to make decisions that cause more pleasure in your society than pain. Accordingly, even if we accept that these so-called choices feel good to the individual, we must examine whether they are good for the society as a whole. The social cost of educated women's decisions to abandon their quest for positions of social power is higher than the benefit to the favored few biological offspring. In other words, they are mostly doing less good than harm. They contribute to perpetuating a mostly male ruling class that will make mistakes; being rulers, those mistakes can be enormous. It is unimaginable that the decisions about abortion and male-only schools would sound the same if there had been no women on the Supreme Court.

The stay-at-home behavior also violates the more good than harm principle because it tarnishes every female with the knowledge that she is almost certainly not going to be a ruler. Princeton President Shirley Tilghman described the elite college's self-image perfectly when she told her freshmen last year that they would be the nation's leaders—and she clearly did not have biking and tree climbing in mind.

It is only a matter of time until people figure out that women aren't a good bet for education and opportunity. Conservatives are already asking why society should spend resources educating women with only a 50 percent return rate on their stated goals. Judge Posner says everyone knows the female students at the fancy law schools aren't going to stay the course. There are now more women in college than men, and tuition doesn't cover the cost of most educations. Taxpayers subsidize their educations, even if the women don't attend overtly tax-supported institutions like state schools. When people give donations to private universities they deduct them from their taxes. Unless the government spends less, the rest of us have to pick up the slack by paying more taxes.

The American Conservative Union carried a column in 2004 recommending that employers stay away from women who are going to cut back or drop out. "But let's say that you, the CEO, did what feminist activists advocate: install a family friendly workplace that prioritizes work-life balance. You might hire lots of people [like women]. If so, your company would likely go out of business."

Good psychological data show that women's ambitions rise and fall in proportion to how much respect they get early on. The more institutions of power, like universities, and employers treat women as if they won't play the game, the more women won't aspire to playing the game. From the standpoint of more good than harm, the opt-out revolution is really a downward spiral.

My female colleagues in the philosophy biz remind me that maybe women have different moral standards from the twenty-five centuries of insights the old white men turned up. The most famous example of this is the work of psychologist Carol Gilligan, who concluded from a study she conducted that women concern themselves more with maintaining a web of relationships among people than with their own individual well-being or a clear set of rules for human behavior. Gilligan's suggestion that females may experience morality differently from males is very controversial, and her study was never replicated. But for our purposes it does not matter. Even Gilligan's "relational" morality was not confined to the nuclear family, but focused on relationships in the larger community.

Here again the homeward bound fail the test of Western morality. Both my interviews and the public debate reflect that women who drop out of the public world demonstrate a singular indifference to the larger society. Maybe it was the intense pressure to create an unheard-of utopia for their children and within the four walls of the single-family dwelling, but when the *Times* brides did do some volunteer work, it was almost always at their children's schools or at churches, where they could look after their children's treatment by making themselves valuable to the school personnel. Several left the schools when their children were finished and followed them to the next school. Again, the social good is concentrated only in a narrow, familial world.

In 1963, Betty Friedan called on society to confront the injustice of the feminine mystique, and the initial reaction was volcanic. It can happen again. Women are people, and people understand when they are being treated unjustly, even by themselves. Neil Chethik's book *VoiceMale—What Husbands Really Think About Their Marriages, Their Wives, Sex, Housework, and Commitment* reveals that men who do more of their share of the housework find their wives more interested in having sex with them. It's not a revolution, for sure, but it's a beginning.

WHAT IS TO BE DONE

Now that we understand what happened and why it's bad, let's make a plan to change it. I have a Strategic Plan to Get to Work. It is a plan to break through the glass ceiling at home, to liberate women to seek flourishing lives and to distribute responsibility for the family fairly between the two adults who created it. The beauty of these solutions is that they do not involve wishful thinking about changing a deeply conservative culture and politics. The plan is focused on the realities of the known domestic world. Indeed, many of them came from the handful of women I found who were succeeding at work and home.

Here are the realities. Men come to the choice intersection with a wallet full of inherited entitlements and women come with a designer bag—of expectations. Consider the story of Deborah Fallows, BA, Harvard, Ph.D., University of Texas, and the author of an early stay-at-home-mom book, *A Mother's Work.* As feminist Joan Williams tells the story in her excellent *Unbending Gender,* Fallows first began to separate from her actual profession when, pregnant with their first child, she followed her husband to Washington, D.C., for his work. After attending Lamaze classes without him (too busy), she gave birth, cut back to part-time work, and then quit completely. When he changed jobs, he tried to shape his job a little to his family life. This was perceived as a huge sacrifice for him: "I have heard him turn down breakfast, dinner, and evening meetings to be with the boys. . . . Many of his friends and colleagues are single or childless. As he sees them sit down for an afternoon of uninterrupted work on a Saturday or Sunday, I can tell he's thinking how much more quickly he could finish an article or book if he were similarly unencumbered. In short, he's made a trade: ambitious as he is, he has accepted less success—and money—than he might otherwise have. In exchange he has gotten to know his sons."

You'd never know it from the tale, but, despite the occasional weekend off, her husband is enormously successful. Mind the heroic terms she uses for his "sacrifice." The media are replete with stories of stay-at-home dads who contend that their decisions mean there is no such thing as a gender ideology about who should care for home and family. Yet in 2004, when the census bureau looked, Mr. Moms comprised a mere 2 percent of the stay-at-home parents, 98,000 out of 5.5 million, and are singularly absent from the ruling class. (My favorite example of this sham refuge of scoundrels from the elite comes from the Web site Tech Central Station: "Seven-time Tour de France champion Lance Armstrong recently retired from bicycle racing in order to, yup, spend more time with his family. Reporters did not bother to press him to explain how divorcing the mother of his children to marry a rock star reflects his commitment to family.")

Why are we so interested in people who comprise 2 percent of the stay-at-home parents? Because any man who does not take full advantage of the gender ideology is tantamount to Hercules? Deborah Fallows's husband and the handful of stay-at-home dads may be heroes to their wives, but—even in her own eyes—Deborah Fallows has done nothing more than what's right. Like Miriam Peskowitz's move to a home eight hours from her academic job, her self-abnegation is as invisible as the air we breathe.

The entitlements and expectations are all the more powerful because they are so hard to see. Once, the entitlements were explicit. In the words of the great eighteenth-century English legal commentator William Blackstone, a man is entitled to the services of his wife because she is inferior, and "the inferior hath no kind of property in the company, care, or assistance of the superior." Real legal chains bound her in the home. She could have little property, not even her own wages. She could not obtain a divorce. Anyone who helped her escape was vulnerable to civil and criminal charges for alienation of affection and other wrongs.

In this way, the first wave of feminism, in the nineteenth century, was lucky because something that explicit and oppressive can be addressed with the familiar language of liberalism—freedom and equality. They enacted Married Women's Property acts, so women could make contracts and keep their wages; and divorce laws; they won the vote; they opened high schools and colleges for girls.

By the time Betty Friedan wrote, the chains of entitlement and expectation had changed. The chains that bound women to the home in Friedan's time were the golden psychological chains of the 1950s, not the iron bands of 1850. Although people love to quote the marriage manuals of the time for language about husbands' "letting" their wives work, women could own property, they could work for wages (they had done so throughout World War II), divorce no longer meant social suicide and loss of child custody.

Friedan's opening salvo, therefore, is not about women's property ownership; it is about suburban housewives' yearning ("the problem that has no name"). Her villains are both tradition and "Freudian sophistication" experts who taught women their worldly aspirations were not illegal, but "neurotic, unfeminine, unhappy."

Who laid these expectations on women? Not storm troopers or judges, but "women's magazines, advertisements, television, movies, novels, columns and books by experts on marriage and the family, child psychology, sexual adjustment and the popularizers of sociology and psychoanalysis." Friedan told women that housework was something simply to be gotten out of the way, marriage an unromantic partnership. Her frustrated housewives were covered with "great bleeding blisters"; they didn't get enough sex, they sought fulfillment in adultery, and their "housewifery was expanding to fill the time available." She noted that Freud and his followers had made mothers indispensable—when children suffered from neuroses or mental illnesses. Husbands who disagreed were looking for substitute mothers.

So off they went. The percentage of women in the full- or part-time workforce rose from 43 percent in 1977 to 59 percent in 2005. The percentage of mothers (of children of any age) who are in the workforce rose from 47 percent in 1975 to 73 percent in 2000. Recessions came and went, but each time the employment rate went back up, the female and maternal employment rate went back up. Good statistical data reflect that women's decisions about working are less and less influenced by the presence or absence of husbands in the household.

But they never lost their chains. Did Stanford Law School's surgeon husband ever consider putting off his surgical residency? The idea that men are entitled to be ideal workers in the market economy and that women are responsible for housekeeping and child rearing survived forty years of feminism without a scratch. The chains just transmuted from golden links into the bonds of the invisible fence, like the one people use to confine their dogs to the yard. This time it was not man's legal right or the woman's natural and healthy destiny; it was her "choice" that laid (or kept) housekeeping and child rearing in her lap.

It's a disempowering choice. In a recent article in the British newspaper *The Guardian,* Suzanne Goldenberg asserted that "constant negotiation might not fit some people's idea of home." But where there is no bargaining, everything does not fall naturally into some utopian, just arrangement. Where there is no bargaining, it's not that no one has the advantage. Where there is no bargaining, the strong rule. Men come to a marriage with the advantages of thousands of years of conventional assumptions that they are entitled to female domestic labor. Blogger Bitch PhD, who is actually a university professor, put her finger on it: "The problem with housework is that it's always the weaker player who's trying to enforce the deal."

According to Phyllis Moen and Patricia Roehling's *Career Mystique,* "When couples marry, the amount of time that a woman spends doing housework increases by approximately 17 percent, while a man's decreases by 33 percent." A study by the University of California faculty revealed that young faculty women with children work thirty-seven hours a week on family care; if they are thirty-four to thirty-eight, they work a self-reported but staggering forty-three hours a week on family care. Young dads work only two thirds as much (twenty-five hours); in the thirty-four to thirty-eight age bracket the gap is even higher—dads work half as hard as their female counterparts. Not surprisingly, childless women make the fastest career advancement in academic jobs; just as fast as childless men. But married men do best of all.

Surely this isn't the fate that women, especially women born in the decades after feminism opened the public world to them, dreamed of. Even if they cherish the prospect of raising children, they rarely articulate a passionate attachment to picking up the dry cleaning. The bizarre disconnect between today's college students who announce in one breath that they are going to be earning six-figure incomes and taking a decade off to raise children testifies to the resilience of the ambitious dream, even against clearly foreseeable odds.

Against this background, women who want to have sex and children with men as well as good work in interesting jobs where they may occasionally wield real social power need guidance, and they need it early. The promises of reduced work hours and government day care, like the prospect of coming back on stream after years away, are just cruel diversions from what *can* be done now. As Salon.com's Rebecca Traister put it, "This debate has in recent years been muffled—out of embarrassment or paralysis in the face of problems so thorny and personal that they are hard to parse, let alone solve. It's about time we all started taking the politics of the American home seriously again, remembering that the personal is absolutely political."

If women's flourishing does matter, the family is to 2006 what the workplace was to 1964 and the vote to 1920. We have taken the first step by simply talking about flourishing. This has angered some, but it should sound the alarm before the next generation winds up in the same situation. Now, how to put the talk into action.

RULES: If I Am Not for Me, Who Will Be for Me?

If your future is ahead of you—or even if you're in the middle of it—there are steps to take right now to move toward a just and flourishing life. No matter what Betty Friedan said, blasting out of traditional roles is not going to be easy. It will require rules—rules like those in the widely derided book *The Rules*, which was never about dating but about behavior modification. Why rules? Because the invisible fence is invisible—but potent—so you need sustain a few shocks to break out of the yard. Because convention is the default position, so you need clear advantages in bargaining. Because loving husbands/fathers don't do the housework unless they must.

There are four rules that should rule your roost: Educate yourself for good work, treat work seriously, don't hamstring yourself when you come to the marital bargaining table, and consider a reproductive strike (one child).

Rule #1: Frida Kahlo Is No Role Model

There has been a lot of press lately about how women are increasingly outnumbering men in undergraduate institutions. Everyone talks about how education is key to success in the postindustrial state. Why aren't these better educated women taking over the rulership of the information economy? Because they're dabbling. It is shocking to think that girls cut off their options for a public life of work as early as college. But they do. The first pitfall is the liberal arts curriculum, which women are good at, graduating in larger numbers than men do. Although many really successful people start out studying liberal arts, the purpose of a liberal education is not, with the exception of a minuscule number of academic positions, job preparation.

I call this the Frida Kahlo problem. Everybody loves Frida Kahlo. Half Jewish, half Mexican, tragically injured when young, sexually linked to men and women, abused by a famous genius husband. Oh, and a brilliantly talented painter. If I was a feminazi, the first thing I'd ban would be books about Frida Kahlo. Because Frida Kahlo's life is not a model for women's lives. And if you're not Frida Kahlo and you major in art, you're going to wind up answering the phones at some gallery in Chelsea, hoping a rich male collector comes to rescue you.

So the first rule is to use your education with an eye to career goals. If feminists really wanted to help you, each year NOW would produce a survey of the most common job op-

portunities for people with college degrees, along with the average lifetime earnings from each job category and the charac-
teristics such jobs require. The point here is to help you see
that yes, you can study art history, but only with the realistic
understanding that one day soon you will need to use your arts
education to support yourself and your family. The survey
would ask young women to select what they are best suited for
and give guidance on the appropriate course of study. Like the
rule about accepting no dates for Saturday after Wednesday
night, the survey would set realistic courses for you, helping
would-be curators who are not artistic geniuses avoid career
frustration and avoid solving their job problems with marriage.

My small survey turned up a disturbing trend that showed
the difference between men and women. All of the *Times*
brides and all of the less privileged women on Blogging
Baby.com had their BAs. But a disturbing number of them
didn't finish graduate or professional school. Or if they did,
they didn't like it and kept going back for more degrees, and
still they were not finding meaningful and prosperous work.
By contrast, every *Times* groom assumed he had to succeed in
business and was really trying. Here's a perfect example of the
difference. One of my *Times* couples, both lawyers, met at a
firm early in their careers. After a few years at an international
law firm, the man moved from international business law into
international business. The woman quit working altogether.
"They told me law school could train you for anything," she
told me. "But it doesn't prepare you to go into business. I
should have gone to business school." Or rolled over and

watched her husband the lawyer using his education in his first few years of work to prepare to go into a related business.

Dreams are great; they fuel young women's ambitions and open their minds to a wealth of possibilities. But dreams are dangerous when, as I often found in my interviews, they become a fantasy about the kinds of intellectual, prestigious, socially meaningful, politics-free jobs worth the dreamer's incalculably valuable presence. My interviewees could not accept the inevitability that their talents were limited and their futures constrained. Do you think this sounds severe? Well, how many women do you know who set out to be painters or writers or do-gooders or weren't quite sure when they graduated what they were going to do? So they bounced around from job to job for a few years, got married, and then dropped out because their work wasn't going so well anyway. And how many *men* do you know who dropped out once they got married?

The solution to the ambition/aptitude problem is not all that elusive: It requires moderation and balance. When the inevitable choice point comes, with work and family on the table, a woman in a good, secure job that is often interesting and provides an income worth protecting is much more likely to come out ahead than a woman who followed her bliss and is temping while she waits for the perfect opportunity she knows is out there. Work may be less than ideal, but staying home with your babies is also a constrained future. Everyone winds up somewhere in the hierarchy. Your education should be a safety net as well as a trapeze.

Rule #2: Take Work Seriously

The second rule if you want to maximize your career options after marriage is that you must treat the first few years of work as an opportunity to lose your capitalism virginity and prepare for good work, which you will then treat seriously. If you are not Frida Kahlo or Mother Teresa, the best way to treat work seriously is to find the money. Money is the marker of success in a market economy; it usually accompanies power, and it enables the bearer to wield power, including within the family. In real terms, this means that if you are well situated on your career track when you are married and have children, you will have more say in the family's decisions—where to live, how to live, where to school your kids—and more opportunity to decide how to pursue your ambitions.

Almost without exception, the brides of the *Times* who opted out graduated with roughly the same degrees as their husbands. Yet somewhere along the way the women made decisions in the direction of less money and less opportunity for promotion. The MBA didn't take her job at the investment bank seriously ("It's only money"), so she got fired. Her next job was with a public relations business consultant, further from the belly of the capitalist beast. A woman with a BA in management met her husband, a BA in management, at the big insurance company where they had both worked since college. When she started, she chose a middle level department, with little upside potential, although she admits that with her degree she could have gotten any entry-level management job. At the same moment in his career, he chose to shoot for international brokerage, where there was more travel but also more money at the top. The lawyer quit her job at the firm while her lawyer husband attended to positioning himself to move over into business. Aim high. Life brings you low soon enough without your help.

Lorna Wendt, the cast-off wife of GE Capital mogul Gary Wendt, who tried to claim in their divorce that she earned half his millions giving dinner parties, graduated the same day he did from Wisconsin. After that, he went to business school, and she became a piano teacher. There's nothing wrong with being a piano teacher, for sure, but not if you think you should live the millionaire's lifestyle she later claimed she earned. If you want it, better try to make it yourself.

Part of the problem is idealism; idealism on the career trail usually leads to volunteer work or indentured servitude in social-service jobs, which is nice but doesn't get you to money. Someone has to do the hard work of holding the society together. I think there should be a law that every teacher in a state should be paid the same salary as the highest earning CEO in the same state.

But in this world, if you are going to choose socially meaningful work over materially rewarding work, there are two things to watch for. One, the work must pay you enough to live on, however modestly. Otherwise, if you are married you're already completely dependent on your husband, or once you get married you'll be under pressure to give it up. Two, the work must mean the world to you. One of the wealthiest women I know runs a hospice. She would no more give that up at the instance of her affluent spouse than die herself. However, just because a job is outside the market economy doesn't mean it will be a good job. Remember: It was a not-for-profit institution, Harvard University, that produced the Kissinger Rule, which he announced after a particularly egregious faculty meeting. The rule is: The less money at stake, the worse the institutional politics are. Be a tough-minded idealist.

Another big mistake is changing jobs excessively. Without exception, the brides who eventually went home had much more job turnover than the grooms had. There's nothing inherently wrong with changing jobs, especially in the direction of better status and pay and opportunity. However, many of the women changed to similar or less prestigious jobs because they could not get along with their co-workers or they kept changing their minds about what they wanted to do. There's no such thing as a perfect job. Condoleezza Rice actually wanted to be a pianist, and pianist Gary Graffman didn't want to give concerts. Don't look to work for a perfect life.

Rule #3: Don't Draw the Short Straw at the Dining-Room Table

Women bid down in the workplace and then they wind up doing the housework. The Center for Work-Life Policy reports that fully 40 percent of highly qualified women with spouses felt that their husbands create more work around the house than they perform. Not a single *Times* groom was a stay-at-home dad. In my interviews, several of them said they could hardly wait for Monday morning to come. None of my *Times* grooms took even brief paternity leave when his children were born. The less privileged women from BloggingBaby.com also bore most of the housework, even the one who was working full time.

Women complain to their girlfriends, but Gary Becker won a Nobel Prize in economics in 1992 because he started explaining how marriage works to produce this divide. Becker asked, What would happen if we thought about marriage like any other kind of human transaction? People would marry if marriage made them better off than not being married, he answered, and they'd select a spouse who would make them better off than the next best candidate. As radical as the idea of applying economic analysis to romance was, Becker then turned quite conventional. After the tough-minded marriage bargain, she'd specialize in housework, according to his theory, and he'd specialize in a paid job. (He started writing about it in 1973.) Specializing, they'd have more stuff, which economists call surplus.

But here's the really interesting question: What happens to that surplus? At that point in the exercise Nobel Laureate Becker morphed into a mommy blogger and suggested that, once married, what his critics call the "husband-father-dictator-patriarch" would be altruistic and feel rewarded when the wife and children were happy. Feeling this way, Becker speculated, dad would offer the family members a division of the marital surplus they would want to take. He would say, "Let's spend half the income I earn [because I don't have to pick up the dry cleaning] on you and half on me." Thus, after the wedding,

Becker's marriage became invisible to economic as well as moral analysis, leaving open the question of whether men actually behave in such a lovely way.

Turns out, they don't. Once Becker opened the bedroom door, an army of other scholars poured in, to examine what really went on inside marriage. Happily, in England, the government did something that enabled people to test Becker's theory that Father Knows Best when it comes to distributing the family assets. In 1979, the English government changed the way it made the welfare payment for poor children. Instead of paying the benefit to the husband at work, the benefit check was mailed to the local post office, where it was usually picked up by the wife and mother during the husband's working hours. After the transfer to the post office, family expenditures on children's clothing went up fifty-four pounds ($95 in 2006 dollars) and expenditures on women's clothing went up by thirty-nine pounds ($68 in 2006 dollars). And the expenditures on men's clothing went down. Other studies of family expenditure uniformly found "a positive relationship between women's share of family income and expenditures on women's and children's clothing." Even after discounting that she might need a big-shouldered suit to wear to work. Women make more bread? Guys buy less pipe tobacco. Guess father's altruism didn't stop him from overindulging at the necktie counter or the tobacco shop after all.

Once the economists shed Becker's quaint notion that people completely change character after they walk down the aisle, they rapidly figured out that the partner who would be better off after an imagined divorce will have greater bargaining power at every point in the marriage itself. Divorce is called, unsentimentally, the threat point. As Terry Martin Hekker's essay in the *New York Times* reflected, in a one-income family, upon divorce the man is generally better off because, even if he gives her the house, he still has his income. (Mr. Hekker went on a cruise with his new honey, and Terry applied for food stamps.) A dozen studies showed this to be true. And so, "If housework is considered undesirable, the spouse with the weaker bargaining position at an imaginary divorce will perform a greater share of the household responsibilities. Since on average the husband has higher earnings, he is better able to purchase market substitutes for home produced goods possibly provided by his wife and thus has a relatively stronger bargaining position."

Worse, women doing housework and husbands making more money is a mutually reinforcing cycle. When you quit work, you lose something called human capital. That's economics talk for your Rolodex—all the current contacts, up-to-date skills, and relevant experience a daily appearance at work produces. As Grossbard-Shechtman put it, "Time spent on home production also directly reduces earnings for women." It doesn't matter where you work or what kind of human capital you accumulate, how many children you have, or whether you are married. Housework up, earnings down. Although no one is sure what causes the effect, Grossbard-Shechtman speculates that it is a devilish combination of reduced energy and attention to the labor market, intermittent disruptions because of the unpredictability of domestic emergencies, and the good old inability to work late when deadlines loom.

By contrast, men enjoy a "marriage premium" of at least 10 percent! Even holding constant for their education and experience, married men earn more than single men. One explanation to date is that their wives are picking up the socks, but one can never completely discount the power of the ideology of gender. Married men may get paid better, because they are doing the job of a man, supporting a family. According to *The Career Mystique* fathers of sons even enjoy a premium over fathers of daughters.

Regardless of what is going on, your "choosing" to shoulder the household at the expense of your market employment means you will be disempowered at divorce. You will therefore be disempowered at every moment before divorce, even if divorce never occurs.

Divorce being sort of the nuclear option, economists quickly developed a model for a marriage worse than Becker's fairy tale but not bad enough to explode. They call it the separate spheres or noncooperative marriage. In this model, each spouse occupies a clearly delineated role within the family, and they bargain from their respective corners. Unlike the cozy Becker marriage, the later model sees the couple repeatedly confronting decisions about who should bear the burdens of child care and housekeeping. Couples have a variety of ways to position themselves in this ongoing negotiation. For example, when they invest in educational credentials, they are strengthening their hand in marital bargaining from the outset with evidence that they can most profitably spend their time at the office.

When we put on the lenses of noncooperative marriage what do they reveal? Remember Miriam Peskowitz's eight-hour commute to work and Deborah Fallows's move to Washington, D.C.? One of economists' favorite indicators of marital bargaining is "location, location, location." Who relocates to serve the other spouse's external earning power is a crucial, and objective, indicator of who's on top. It does not matter whether the spouse who wants to move promises future good behavior, because there are no sure punishments if s/he reneges on the promise. Once a spouse moves to a place of the other spouse's work and away from her work, her hand in future negotiations over who serves the family is weakened. Thanks to the unlikely assistance of the conventionally conservative discipline of economics, we can see what the deal is.

What to do? If you are single, here are some strategies available to you. First, be aware of your bargaining power in courtship. Very recent studies of marriage reflect that people seek spouses who resemble them in education and class. "Like marries like," the work/family scholar Francine Blau put it to me in an interview. As the *Times* marriage announcements reflect, leaving aside Donald Trump, the old businessman and the showgirl business is totally passé. Similar current work reveals that men are more eager to wed than women are. So pay no attention to *Newsweek* magazine's suggestion that you are more likely to be killed by a terrorist than find a husband. Educated, gainfully employed women are a valuable commodity. If you can make clear before you commit that you will not quit work to care for the household even if you have children, it will set the context for the later bargaining, even if it doesn't guarantee a good outcome. Don't sell yourself short.

If you are uncertain about your resolve, you can look for

a spouse with less social power than you, or an ideological commitment to gender equality, or a high tolerance for squabbling. In her 1995 book, *Kidding Ourselves: Babies, Breadwinning and Bargaining Power*, Rhona Mahoney recommended finding a sharing spouse by marrying down—younger or poorer, or someone in a dependent status, like a starving artist. As one of my few working *Times* brides told me, the first rule is never marry a Wall Street type. Because money is such a marker of status and power, it's hard to persuade women to marry poorer. So here's an easier rule: Marry young or marry much older.

Younger men are potential high-status companions. Much older men are sufficiently established so that they don't have to work so hard, and they often have enough money to provide generous household help. By contrast, slightly older men with bigger incomes are the most dangerous to a workingwoman's domestic power. If you both are going through the elite-job hazing rituals simultaneously while having children, someone is going to have to give. Even the most devoted lawyers with the hardest working nannies are going to have weeks when no one can get home other than to sleep. The odds are that when this happens, the woman is going to give up her ambitions and professional potential.

You might think that marrying a liberal might be the better course. After all, conservatives justified the unequal family in two modes: "God ordained it" and "biology is destiny." Most men (and most women), including the liberals, think women are responsible for the home. But at least the liberal men should feel squeamish about it. In a completely unscientific survey, men on conservative Web sites responding to the suggestion that women lose their chains do tend to invoke the Bible and the law of nature more often than liberal Web sites. Liberal men tend to make arguments about how lucky they are that their wives happened to choose to stay home or how awful it is to work in heartless capitalism. But the result is the same.

If you are already married, it will take more fortitude, but just don't make the bad deals the economics literature has identified. The most common kinds of bad deals come in two forms: economics and home economics. The economic trap is to assign the cost of child care to the woman's income. If it takes two people to make a baby, why is the cost of child care the woman's burden alone? If couples, yes, even liberal couples, would stop following this path, it would make a gender revolution all by itself.

Here's what the bad bargain looks like: If a woman making $50,000 per year whose husband makes $100,000 decides to have a baby, and the cost of a full-time nanny is $30,000, the couple reasons that, after paying 40 percent of her own salary in taxes, the woman makes $30,000, just enough to pay the nanny. So she might as well stay home. This totally ignores the fact that both adults are in the enterprise together and the demonstrable future loss of income, power, and security for the woman who quits. Instead, calculate that all workers in the family make a total of $150,000 and take home $100,000 after paying their average tax bill. After paying a full-time nanny, they have $70,000 left to live on.

The home-economics trap is housework. My solutions are ignorance and dust. Never figure out where the butter is. "Where's the butter?" Nora Ephron's legendary riff on marriage begins. In it, a man asks the question when looking directly at the butter container in the refrigerator. "Where's the butter?" actually means butter my toast, buy the butter, remember when we're out of butter. Next thing you know you're quitting your job at the law firm because you're so busy managing the butter. If women never start playing the household-manager role, the house will be dirty, but the realities of the physical world will trump the pull of gender ideology.

But a big piece of the puzzle has to be that women must give up control. You may think you know how to diaper better than your husband, how to load the dishwasher better than your husband, how to read the labels on your clothes going into the wash better than your husband. And you may be *right*. You *are* better. But ask yourselves about the trade-off— one T-shirt turned pink because it went into the darks wash versus a lifetime of doing the wash yourself. And then work hard to let your husband run the dishwasher with only six plates in it, as long as you don't have to do it all.

The Blogger Bitch PhD, who is a working mother, has another promising approach. She advises, "Don't fuck around with 'housework strikes'—it'll drive you crazy before it does him, probably, and you'll cave. Don't get stuck in arguments about 'who cares more' or . . . 'I'll do whatever you ask me to'—all of which are excuses that mean 'I don't think it's my responsibility to do housework, so of course I care less/don't bother/don't notice/will 'help' if you think for me and tell me what to do." Bitch advises, "Go ahead and do what needs to be done. But let him know what you are doing every goddamn step of the way, and let him know that it pisses you off. 'I've just gotten home from work, it's nice to see you're home earlier than I am. Before I take off my coat, I'll put your shoes away for you, shall I? Oh, and I'll pick up your coat from the floor and hang it up. Okay, now I can take off my own coat and hang it up right away, instead of dropping it on the floor for someone else to pick up later. I see there's no dinner started, I'll just get on that shall I? First, though, I'll clear the mail off the dining room table where you seem to have dropped it when you walked in the door. I'll file it over here where it belongs. Ok, now I'm going to go into the kitchen to get a sponge to wipe off the table, which I see hasn't been wiped since breakfast—I guess you didn't have a chance to do that yet, since you had to sit down and read the paper first, right? Wow, now that I'm in the kitchen, I see that before I can start dinner I have to load the dishwasher, but before I can do that I have to unload it. . . .'"

Without any reference to the economic literature about willingness to divorce, she seems to intuit the bottom line: "If you do that for a week or so, both of you will start to notice how much work is being done, and how unfair the distribution is. And both of you will have to make a decision. You will have to decide if doing this much extra work, every day for the rest of your life, is something you're willing to do to keep the marriage going. And he will have to decide if he is willing to listen to you bitch at him about it for the rest of his life, or if it would be easier to get up off his ass and do his fair share, *or if he is so unwilling to get up off his ass that he would rather divorce you than be forced to notice how unfair he's being* [emphasis added]. That's the bottom line, and I recommend figuring out where it is sooner rather than later, and deciding whether or not you can live with it."

If this sounds a little like Edward Albee's famous portrayal of marital unhappiness, *Who's Afraid of Virginia Woolf,* with its endless posturing, betrayal, and renegotiation, you can see why people would just give up and do what's conventional. Economists call giving in to convention avoiding the transaction costs of bargaining.

If there is a villain in this story of the role of conventional gender roles, it is the weight of history. Western traditions, and particularly Western religions, value female chastity. As anthropologist Helen Fisher tells us, "Early peoples of the Tigris–Euphrates valley felt that a woman had to 'maintain her virtue.' A wife who was adulterous could be executed or have her nose chopped off. Meanwhile, a husband had license to fornicate with prostitutes whenever he chose; philandering was a transgression only if he coupled with another man's wife or took the virginity of a peer's eligible daughter." Accordingly, there is a long tradition of sequestering women in various ways, usually in an extended family. Historian Stephanie Coontz tells us that later, modern capitalism and liberal politics threatened to dissolve all such human bonds. In response, the ideal of the romantic family, with its male breadwinner and altruistic dependent female, really took off. Finally, women bear children and nurse them. Before reliable birth control and extended life expectancy, a woman's life could consist of bearing and nursing children, one after another for three decades. Women died in childbirth—before 1750 at roughly 150 times the modern rate. Religion, private property, fertility, life expectancy. A pattern is laid down. It becomes convention.

This is the final hurdle. Even if you are, like Blogger Bitch PhD, a wife and mother, committed to your work and working at a good job (she's a college professor), you will still face the transaction costs of bargaining away from the conventional arrangement. You will not have happy days or weeks while applying Blogger Bitch PhD's housework narrative to your household. I must, however, confess that I have been trying her method myself recently with some results.

Rule #4: Use Reproductive Blackmail

In 2001, when Patty Ireland stepped down as head of NOW, she told the *Washington Post*—with regret but apparently without irony—that she had never had children because "I decided that I couldn't do what I wanted to do with my career and have children." This is extreme. And a little sad. Have a baby. *Just don't have two.* In the midst of an important new analysis of the effect of tax policy on marriage, the prominent economic analyst of marriage, Robert Pollak, describes childbearing as "a big, up-front decision that affects future bargaining power" as follows: "A husband's promise to share equally in child care is unenforceable and, recognizing this, a couple may have fewer children than both spouses would prefer." (Somehow, even Pollak, who saw right through the altruistic father gambit awhile back, does not worry that a wife's child-care behavior might require enforcing. Maybe that's because monkeys do it but, once again, the woman's work is rendered invisible.)

The solution to male reneging is the reproductive strike. Judith Statdman Tucker, editor and founder of the Web-based activist organization Mothers Movement Online, reports that women who opt out of work for child-care reasons generally act only after the second child arrives. A second kid pressures the mother's organizational skills; doubles the demands for appointments; wildly raises the cost of child care, education, and housing; and drives the family to the suburbs. (Cities, with their Chinese carryouts and all, are better for working mothers.)

So don't be a Gary Becker booby. Every time a woman quits, she reduces her human capital for some future venture into the labor market. There is almost no payoff in the market economy to spending years biking and singing and listening to NPR. Weakened in the outside job market, she is weakened in the marriage. Every time the dishwasher needs to be emptied. If you don't believe me, ask all those men's stores in England whose sales plummeted when the women started getting the welfare money.

LASHING BACK

I wrote the article "Homeward Bound" to make the argument against women with options opting for home, or at least to open the terms of the debate over this important social issue. I never dreamed that a faculty member of a respectable law school would frame a critique of my work with "Linda Hirshman makes me vomit." And follow it up with "F.U., Linda Hirshman, feminists can say whatever they want." Or that a published author with a Ph.D. would chime in with "Oh, please. She only wants to get a contract to write a book," not normally a bad plan for someone with a Ph.D. and a new idea. An enterprising blogger gathered all the negative responses and entitled the compendium "Everybody Hates Linda." It is worth thinking about why the mothers' defense was so hysterical. When Danielle Crittenden suggested in 2005 to every workingwoman in America that her days' efforts amounted to no more than a "pile of pay stubs," people like Madeleine Albright and Condoleezza Rice did not rush to their computers to tell Crittenden she makes them vomit.

Response also poured in from conservative men, most notably syndicated columnist David Brooks, and a bunch of scary types on the Internet. Taken together, the criticisms of my argument pretty much summarize the whole state of debate about women after feminism; no matter how vociferously they are argued, they aren't very convincing.

Probably the most interesting thing about the counterarguments is the way they illustrate how close conservatives and liberals are when the outcome is keeping women at home. Keep this crucial insight in mind. Liberal critics have accused me of taking the spotlight off employers and legislators, who should be providing women with day-care centers and tax breaks. But those solutions have never happened. One reason they never happened is that such change can certainly never come out of the unspoken liberal/conservative agreement that women probably should do the child rearing and housekeeping.

The arguments fall into three big categories—the "usual suspects" of political debate. They are no argument (you may not criticize women's decisions), no alternatives (the decisions are determined by God or Darwin), and no problem (the decisions are good).

NO ARGUMENT

Most effectively, people argue that you can't argue about women's decisions to abandon the workplace for the home. First, they say it's not happening. Women and mothers are working in as high percentages as ever, critics like liberal economist Heather Boushey say, and any falloff is from the recession of 2000–2004. In another version of "it's not happening," they say women are just sequencing and will come back to even better jobs soon. This is the most liberal response, because it contends that feminism really worked, and all the stories about stay-at-home moms are just wishful thinking from a sexist mainstream media designed to make women change their minds and leave work.

Boushey, like all economists, tries to exclude from the equation a lot of factors that I think are meaningful in an effort to isolate the pure fact of motherhood. She neutralizes the effect of the increasing numbers of Hispanics in the workforce on the grounds that if Hispanic women are staying home, their behavior is dictated by their adherence to a more conventional Hispanic culture of keeping women in the home, rather than the pure fact of motherhood. This is itself debatable in second-generation immigrants but, even if true, it is meaningful if feminism failed to convert new immigrants to a preexisting cultural norm of women working. America, a nation of immigrants, has always exerted a strong pull on immigrant culture. If feminism is not affecting Hispanic mothering patterns, then those are data we need to have.

The same argument applies to ruling out the increase in families with a father in the house. "Pure" motherhood almost never exists, so it's unlikely it will ever account for women's workplace behavior alone. In any event Boushey attributes the falloff in working mothers to the falloff in female employment generally, due to the recession. By that analysis, the percentage of working mothers should have gone up from 2003 to 2004, when employment went up, but it did not. It stayed the same. Other economists have criticized Boushey's numbers because the falloff started before the recession of 2000.

Boushey candidly admits that her analysis does not explain the behavior of women with graduate and professional degrees, such as the *New York Times* brides. At the least, their workforce participation has leveled off for more than five years of sampling. The eruption from the blogs also suggests that, contra Boushey, the stay-at-home behavior goes much deeper than the class of the *Times*. In any event, I have a test for this. Ask yourself, dear reader, about the women you know. Are your friends, with postgraduate educations or not, having babies and dropping out? If you are older, are your children? Their friends? Everywhere I go people stop me with stories of their dropout daughters. Does this resonate with you, too?

Next, liberal critics say you can't argue about women's dropping out, because it's not "helpful" to criticize women.

New York Times ideas editor Patricia Cohen suggested that political criticism of women's actions was dogmatic and passé, a sentiment echoed in their published letters to the editor ("The problem with this new version of the 'mommy wars' is that it takes the heat off the real problem: workplaces out of whack with today's workers, and a society that doesn't value families") and in their guest columnist Judith Warner's blog on the *Times* Web site ("The fix for this solution isn't to pile onto women by preaching to them, one way or the other, about what they must do").

It may make people, especially liberals, mad, but without political analysis and critique, there can be no change. This latest exercise in liberal political correctness is like the laws that prohibited employers from assigning women overtime before the second wave of feminism in the 1960s, a special protection only women got. It really says that women can never hope to debate their situation long enough to rise above it, just like they couldn't work the overtime to be promoted. Or maybe just that women aren't important enough to fight about.

But what if women are a big part of the "real" problem? Ellen Bravo has been advocating family leave and day care for thirty years. Meanwhile, women who could have changed the content and structure of public and market governance are pushing strollers around on the Upper West Side of New York City. Mommy bloggers and authors are telling the less fortunate ones that they just need to give up their big-screen TVs and stuff and stay home. Picture a world in which women pursued their careers, refused to marry men who wouldn't fully participate in running the household, and refused to have more than one child. If they had done that, would we still be living in a society that does not "value families"?

A narrower argument is that, even if you could criticize women, you can't criticize women when they're in the family. Conservatives, who assert that God created the nuclear family or that Darwin did, understandably embrace this position, but the blindness to justice in the family crosses political lines. Liberal Judith Warner calls the family an "all but hopeless conundrum," something that, by definition, cannot be solved. But what is there about the cooperative venture of two adults that makes it insoluble? Women have made a set of bad bargains. There's no structural reason they could not make a better one. That's what all the economic analysis of marriage is about.

The family would pose a dilemma if, as some have proposed, marriage and bargaining for a fairer distribution could not coexist. That would mean that people stay in love only with spouses who agree to do exactly as the other wants them to. How many people do you know who are such complete doormats? Even the welfare-dependent, unemployed mothers in Great Britain, when they got their hands on the child subsidies from the post office, spent the money on things their husbands would not buy—clothing for themselves and for the children. There was no report of a spike in the English divorce rate when this disagreement surfaced.

In an interview, "Mommy Wars," author Miriam Peskowitz told me the family should be excluded from any discussion of women's lives, because it's so complex and difficult. I have an easy test to tease out what this family immunity from scrutiny business really means. "What if the husband beats up on the wife?" I ask. "That's behind the four walls of the single-family dwelling." Invariably, the family-is-private bunch fail the test. "Oh, I didn't mean violence!" Peskowitz said in her interview. So now we see it's not that the family is immune from moral analysis; it's that we think women bearing 70 percent of housekeeping is just. Or at least one of those choices like chocolate or vanilla, which don't rise to the level of moral scrutiny. And this is the liberal position.

The broader liberal position is that you can't criticize the choices anyone makes at all regardless of their sex. If the decision to stay home with the kiddies is automatically right just because some woman chose it, then we should not be wasting any more time debating it. It is important to remember that the idea that choice is sacrosanct originated around the seventeenth century, mostly as a justification for resisting a state-imposed religious belief, after centuries of religious warfare. Although saving someone's soul is definitely a value, the advocates of choice at the time noted that it's hard to argue with someone who talks to God. They also noticed that the people trying to save your soul, say by killing or torturing you, might have an ulterior motive, like wanting to take your property. The persistence of religious disagreement made it very unlikely that the bloodshed would ever stop and that one side or the other might be wrong about salvation. So for some time in the West, off and on, people agreed to stop using the state to impose their *religious* choices on one another.

If we can generalize beyond the context of religious freedom, there is a broader argument that people's choices for their own lives are entitled to respect, whether they involve religion or not. We care about humans, because we think they have the capacity for free will. (That's why we say people "deserve" punishment when they do wrong.) People choosing do have a better, finer-grained understanding of all the facts, as they are right on the scene. If they feel they have imposed it on themselves, they are likely to be committed to it and efficient in executing the plan. These are all good reasons for not using the coercive machinery of the state to dictate peoples' choices for their lives except where necessary. (The most common justification for coercion is harm to others, like murder.) And this is where the discussion usually ends.

But, hey, wait a minute. People choose to do all kinds of things that are questionable, if not plain wrong. They don't fasten their seat belts. They build McMansions in historic villages. They take dangerous drugs. They grind down their workers' wages. Just because you can't put someone on the rack for something doesn't make it right. It just means that, on balance, the cost—mistake, corruption, disrespect—of having the state stop them is too great. Somewhere along the way, the idea that the state shouldn't dictate all behavior unnecessarily got translated into the idea that all behavior is morally equal, what the conservatives correctly castigate as "relativism." And criticizing someone's behavior becomes the equivalent of sending them to the gas chamber.

But of course this is nonsense. As we discussed in an earlier section, every time someone votes, they make choices about the kind of society they want to live in, and they are willing to use their numbers to impose that choice on the others in the

society. Otherwise, they'd be anarchists or something and refuse to participate in governing, even by voting. And people
give advice—gratuitous or solicited—to their friends and families, and they gossip and judge the people they know and the
movie stars they don't know. They decide O. J. Simpson killed
his wife and belongs in prison. They judge.

The trick is to have standards by which the choices can be
judged. In America, the void created by relativism was a clear
invitation to religion. And religious organizations, mostly Western monotheism of various sorts, with its entire history of male
dominance and female subservience, have happily stepped up
to the plate. But just as doing God's will is not the only reason
for humans to lead good lives, so religion is not the only
source for standards by which choices can be judged. As we
saw in our dalliance with the dead white men, there is an ancient tradition in the West of judging lives for their fidelity to
a standard of full humanity, without regard to the divine.
Does it use your human capacities to the fullest? Does it carve
out the maximum space for independence? Does it do more
good than harm?

So there are standards for judging that don't involve talking
to God, and there are lots of ways to advocate your judgments
other than a religiously driven inquisition. But if choice is
trumps, you never even get to start the conversation. No
change can occur, so a seemingly liberal argument has an illib-
eral result. It is not surprising, therefore, that the most conservative players in the feminist world embrace the concept of
choice. The Independent Institute, a conservative organization funded in part by Microsoft to resist the government's

antitrust suit, and also the source of a publication defending smoking, recently published a collection of essays, purportedly politically inclusive, called *Liberty for Women.* Here's its seductive offer to "feminism for the 21st century . . . Choice is the key, and every woman's choices and expressions of self-ownership must be equally and legally respected, from housewives to CEOs. Only then can a meaningful debate arise over which choices may be the best ones for women to make freely." The conservative "feminists" of the Independent Institute apparently missed the last twenty-five years of choice. The dirty little secret is that, if they have their way, the debate will never arise.

The other place the choice argument loses is if the choice is actually an illusion, as it often is. So in the old Jack Benny routine, a thief puts a gun to Benny's head and asks the legendarily tight Benny for his money or his life. A silence ensues. After several seconds, Benny says, "I'm thinking, I'm thinking." What kind of "choice" is this? I have contended that the gender ideology that lays the responsibility for housekeeping on women plays the role in the women's choices like the gun in the Jack Benny gag. It raises the cost of making a decision against ideology so high that the scope of freedom, which dignifies the choices, is greatly reduced.

For all of those reasons, the invitation to leave one another alone is really an invitation to leave the current unjust arrangement in place.

NO ALTERNATIVE

Here and there, someone—usually a conservative—took the bait and tried to address the substance of my moral argument, instead of ducking it with relativism. This requires them to argue that women opting out is the moral choice. A liberal variant of this argument is the argument that work sucks, especially if you make a lot of money at it, so home is relatively better if not actually good.

The oldest substantive argument is probably that God created the "traditional" family and enjoined women to submission. A lot of the argument against my call for women to return to the public sphere came from various religious sources. As long as they don't try to use the state to impose their ways, or hide their religious agenda as innocent, neutral-sounding advice my answers are easy and they are no different from the answers the founders of modern democracy gave to the Church centuries ago. "Maybe you saw Jesus [as so-called feminist Naomi Wolf recently contended]," Thomas Hobbes timidly ventured in 1650, when the Church really could have sent him to the stake. "Or maybe you were only dreaming." How is anyone to argue with someone who talks to God? Maybe their motives are corrupt, greedy, power seeking. How would you know? But there really is no argument against it. If conservatives want to tell women—and women want to believe—that God told them to stay at home, certainly I'm not about to say God told me to tell you to go to work.

Oddly, sometimes the God squad also resorts to Darwin to argue that women "naturally" belong at home. Now, since many of them are rabidly opposed to Darwinian concepts of natural history everywhere else, the exception is suspicious.

The argument that women naturally belong at home, however, has astonishing appeal across the political spectrum. Conservative columnist David Brooks used it in his New Year's Day column to prove definitively that I was "wrong." Evolutionary psychology remains the skeleton in the Carol Gilligan relational feminism closet, deny it though she may. And why not? Western feminism opened the public life to women; half of the ones best situated to take advantage of the opportunity are found at home when their children are small, and the less privileged ones articulate a frustrated desire to join them. Even when working, women in the heterosexual, two-parent family do 70 percent of the household labor. Maybe it is a natural compulsion.

So here's the basic argument, according to two of its most influential academic advocates, anthropology professors Leda Cosmides and John Tooby (*Evolutionary Psychology: A Primer*): The brain is a computer. Its circuits are designed to generate behavior that is appropriate to your environmental circumstances. Our computerlike brains were designed by natural selection to solve problems that our ancestors faced during our species' evolutionary history. Our modern skulls house a Stone Age mind. For this reason, evolutionary psychology is relentlessly past oriented. Cognitive mechanisms that exist because they solved problems efficiently in the past will not necessarily generate adaptive behavior in the present.

Although evolutionary psychology can predict many behaviors, its advocates are particularly focused on sexual behavior. People argue that women naturally seek high-status men and men naturally seek women with clear skin. EPers assert that women have physical brains designed by natural selection to ensure survival of their types during the Stone Age. They are "programmed" by evolution to care for their offspring, who are few and precious, whereas men can spread their sperm around and have many offspring and so are not. Even male chimps are faithless. The rest of it—housekeeping, cooking, and the like—is offshoots of the basic nesting circuit. Trying to change women's behavior is hopeless, because of the power of the evolutionary script. Or as the insight, variously attributed to Dorothy Parker and a bunch of other writers, goes:

> *Hogamus, higamus*
> *Men are polygamous;*
> *Higamus, hogamus*
> *Women, monogamous.*

Many things flowed from this: Monkey behavior suddenly took center stage; old, racist theories of the evolutionary superiority of white people crept out, the (then) president of Harvard said, "Math is hard" for women; and some scientist purported to find a "gay" gene.

Critics of evolutionary psychology contended that the genetic and neurological structure of social behavior was so diffuse and so complex that it was impossible to reduce to a simple structural explanation, like a "gene" for child care. One recent critic, philosopher of science David Buller, provided a compendium of the criticisms in his book *Adapting Minds: Evolutionary Psychology and the Persistent Quest for Human Nature.* He argues that we can't specify the adaptive problems precisely enough to know what kinds of mechanisms would have had to evolve. Challenges were constantly changing because humans create their environment. Buller adds that even if our ancestors did evolve a solution to some problem we may not be able to figure out the solution from the problem. In other words, evolutionary psychological analysis is pure guesswork. The brain is, in fact, a general-purpose problem solver.

The best we can say at present is that there are reasons to be suspicious of the natural hausfrau scenario. First, like talking to God, it leaves no room for counterargument. Second, unlike ordinary evolutionary theory, evolutionary psychology is very difficult to falsify, or disprove. Structural changes driven by natural selection leave a fossil record and other evidence, but Stone Age behavior leaves few traces to test scientifically. The late paleontologist Stephen Jay Gould called it a "just so story."

Indeed, when the EP types have predicted behavior, it has not held up very well (Buller claims he refuted their prediction that stepparents would kill their stepchildren) or has been tainted by culture (women are poorer, so is seeking a richer man genetic or cultural?). Scientists did not find a gene for homosexuality; what they discovered were data suggesting some influence of one or more genes on one particular type of sexual orientation in one group of people, neither a necessary nor a sufficient cause. The study has never been replicated by other researchers, the necessary standard of scientific proof. There's even a communal, bisexual, universally faithless monkey, the bonobo. Female bonobo polygamous.

There are other obvious arguments. It is difficult to go from the child-care argument, which is at least tied to a real physical condition, childbearing, to picking up the socks. About half of American mothers still work full time outside the home, even when the alternative is well short of starvation. So if women are programmed, as conservatives contend, to stay home with their children and keep house, there's an awful lot of unnatural activity going on.

Probably the most important thing to note about the monkey explanation is that although it's a very fragile argument, it completely eliminates any moral discussion about why women aren't participating fully in activities normally associated with good lives. It's easy to see why conservatives love evolutionary psychology: It totally protects whatever status quo exists at the moment. What's more puzzling is why liberals embrace it but, suspiciously, only when it comes to women. The wildly successful popularizer of EP, Richard Dawkins ("Darwin's Rottweiler" by *Discover* magazine), was part of a group of British intellectuals campaigning for John Kerry from afar in 2004. American evolutionary psychology writer Robert Wright similarly presents himself as a liberal. Race-based EP, like conservative Charles Murray's book *The Bell Curve,* makes them wild. But binding women to the home not so much.

NO PROBLEM

People argue that I am wrong about the content of a flourishing life being using your capacities in complex and socially visible enterprises. When they write to me, the homebodies, like the merry maid in the treetops with NPR on her Ipod and a letter to her congressman in her overalls, paint a romantic picture of flourishing in the domestic sphere. As we have already seen, the diaries of the women who live it reflect quite a different set of facts. I'm always worried about a flourishing life in which men refuse to participate.

Since they are, largely, not homeward bound, the substantive liberal male objections to my argument generally take the form of denigrating the world of work. First, they characterize high-powered jobs as taking soul-destroying hours—the current front runner seems to be an incredible eighty hours a week. Professed "economist, dad, spouse" Tom Pozzo of Madison, Wisconsin, describes the world of work in his blog, posting "The Eighty-Hour Work Week: No Thank You." He says, "There are several angles that are worth working when considering the imperative to work as much as you can work, including the likeness of many high-hours work situations to fraternity hazing." From a distance, the mommies, too, see "80-hour weeks required for corporate success."

The U.S. Bureau of Labor Statistics reported in 2000, however, that "weekly hours data for [managers and professionals] . . . show that the average workweek has been about 42 hours during the entire decade and, in fact, has shown little variation since 1982." True, of the men employed as managers and professionals, about four in ten worked at least forty-nine hours per week, twice the share among women. But "these proportions rose steadily during the 1980s, but showed no further increase in the 1990s." The business magazine *Fast Company* says that top business leaders work typically sixty to seventy-five hour weeks. It's a lot of hours, God knows, but it's only the ones at the very top and it's still not the eighty so beloved of bloggers.

Obviously, longer is not the same as soul destroying. An amazing number of bloggers describe their jobs in harrowing terms. "Everyone really hates the workplace. And women and men who poke fun at the women who drop out are just jealous." At the educational level of the *Times* couples, however, the men uniformly reported themselves to be quite happy with their work—the international relations Ph.D. at a fancy New York political consulting firm, the heir to a real estate fortune running a successful commercial real estate brokerage house, the sports nut being the lawyer for Madison Square Garden. We know that many women work even though, with heroic financial sacrifice, they could live on one salary.

No one doubts that there is bad work in the market economy. But it seems extremely unlikely that all the jobs in the public world are soul-destroying tyrannies or that all home life is a bucolic paradise. If that was so, why would men so willingly accept exile? Objectors say that men are pressured into working all those hours by social expectations of them. But can it be that while women are so resolute that they "choose" domestic life without suffering any pressure from the centuries of gender ideology, men are so vulnerable to the social pressure to work that they work at the peril of their souls? And remember, most women—even mothers—still work, even if they would not starve otherwise. So how bad can work really be?

The slobbovniks who write in to complain that they can never satisfy their wives' standards for cleanliness and child safety actually provide a more coherent explanation for why men cling so tenaciously to the world of public work: They don't think housework matters. The one portion of "Homeward Bound" everyone agrees about is that most men don't notice when housework and child care need to be done, don't take responsibility without being assigned, don't complete assignments when they come in, and regard the most trivial contribution as heroic. The commentator who considers the family an unsolvable "conundrum" spends the rest of her column describing how men won't share the family labor, putting women at a terrific disadvantage in the workplace. In sum, work may be soul destroying, but men are voting with their feet that housework is worse!

Conservatives and even some liberals contend that children do better with stay-at-home moms than in day care, yet the liberals propose various schemes like public or market day care to enable women to work all or part time. Just to address the underlying contention, I had planned to make history by being the first feminist ever to write a book that does not contend that children do okay in day care. If, in fact, children need a parent tending to them constantly, that still does not dictate that it must be the mother, with attendant cost to the content of a good life for her. But the critics assert that, on the utilitarian scale of doing more good than harm, the marginal good they add to their own children's well-being outweighs any contribution to the public weal. For this to be true, it must be that children are robustly better off with stay-at-home moms than with working parents.

There certainly are no data for this. When I was on broadcast TV recently, the woman representing full-time mothers produced the devastating fact that the teachers at her children's kindergarten said they could tell immediately which children had stay-at-home moms and which were the deprived subjects of day care. Strangely, the identical story appeared on a Christian Web site as if it happened to someone else. Verbatim.

Turning away from urban legends, then, the only reliable, long-term study has concluded that "out-of-home child care does not appear to damage children's cognitive development or their social and emotional skills." The headlines stem from findings of the National Institute of Child Health and Human Development (NICHD) Study of Early Child Care, published in a series of papers starting in 1993. The NICHD study is the largest and, many say, most comprehensive longitudinal study of child care conducted in the United States. Later NICHD studies indicated that children from middle-class homes may be more disobedient and restless in the early years when they spend more than six hours a day at day care and that the mother/child bond may be slightly weaker, although they have more skills and learning. Certainly there is nothing to indicate that children are significantly worse off. Recent reports reflect that contemporary working mothers spend as much time with their children as stay-at-home moms did in 1975. In any event, if children did need more parenting, in my scheme fathers would have to do half the work of child rearing, so day care could be significantly reduced, and even if mothers took some time out while their only child is young, they could return to the workforce before their human capital was significantly reduced.

Taken altogether, however, this is a daunting collection of opponents. Unlike most social change movements, women, who, like Deborah Fallows, are often the stay-at-home wives of liberal men, face destructive suggestions from the left as well as the right. Luckily, there is a model for a social movement that can confront these powerful opponents and make real social change: gay rights.

EVERYTHING I KNOW I LEARNED FROM THE GAY MOVEMENT

Next season, the cable channel for women is going to launch its version of *Queer Eye for the Straight Guy*, *Feminist Pal for the Opt-Out Gal*. Each episode, a team of three feminists—one an employment market analyst, the second, a job trainer, and the third, an economist specializing in marital bargaining—is going to take on a present or would-be full-time stay-at-home mom and redo her life. From spit-up-covered overalls to Armani business suits! From unemployable philosophy major to intellectual property lawyer! From behind the harem wall in oil man hubby's Arab emirate to a condo in Chelsea! The femgals will revise the SAHM's major, thicken her skin in the work-place, and teach her how to just say no to assignments in Yemen. Having your own health insurance is the new black.

Hard to imagine, isn't it?

How did feminism lose the battle for the hearts and minds? How did the lesbian and gay movement do so well? Both were part of the overall liberation movement of the midtwentieth century. Illinois, the first state to decriminalize consensual sodomy, did so in 1962, just a year before the publication of *The Feminine Mystique*. Both found roots in the leftiest of union and political organizations (Betty Friedan's socialist origins are well known; the founders of the Mattachine Society for homosexuals were ex-Communists). Both invoked well-established American political commitments to liberty in the form of sexual privacy and equality in the form of nondiscrimination.

There are many differences, of course. People who are gay or lesbian are not defined by their role in the reproductive family. The heterosexual white men who run the society are unlikely to offer gay—or lesbian—people a haven from the hardship of carving out a place in the hostile, public world, in the form of a hierarchical home life. And if you push a drag queen hard enough, eventually s/he's going to take a swing at you, precipitating three days of rioting outside of Stonewall in 1969.

But the biggest difference is this: after AIDS, gay activists—probably not even consciously—stopped talking about choice. As journalist and AIDS activist John-Manuel Andriote put it in an interview when his book, *Victory Deferred*, was published in 1999, "As the numbers of gay men killed by AIDS grew to an alarming level, and as the gay community saw early on that AIDS was being neglected because of the hatred of homophobic politicians, they recognized that gay pride and liberation were about more than the right to have sex with whomever they chose. . . . AIDS happened and it profoundly altered the gay civil rights movement as well as the lives of individual gay (and non-gay) people. Period."

Just in time, too. The high-water mark of choice in the gay movement came with the four dissenting votes in the 1986 Supreme Court case *Bowers v. Hardwick,* which reaffirmed the state of Georgia's right to prosecute gay men for criminal sodomy. Although the court's two decades of decisions forbidding the criminalization of every variant of heterosexual practices clearly dictated the opposite outcome, the court simply dug in its heels and said no. Homosexual sodomy is different, the majority ruled. Always been outside the fence. Enraged, the dissenters produced two different opinions about why homosexual sodomy is not different. Each of them relied entirely on the concept that both practices involve choice ("the freedom of an individual to choose the form and nature of these intensely personal bonds" from Justice Blackmun and "the interest in deciding how he will live his own life" from Justice Stevens).

Sadly, the AIDS epidemic provided an unparalleled opportunity to switch from choice to values. As gay men began to die, the people who loved them began to grieve and to write about the nature and content of their relationships, to make the moral claim for full human lives for themselves. Because most laws regarding death are centered in the traditional family, gay men had to fight for every aspect of family life—to stay in their shared homes, to bury their loved ones. Interestingly, the development dovetailed with developments in the lesbian community, which was just beginning its alliance with gay men. Lesbians, who had been fighting to retain custody or visitation after divorces, began going to court to get the families they were creating with donor insemination recognized.

The antisodomy laws allowing the state to throw people in jail for moral relationships, which had just been upheld by the Supreme Court, began to seem not just a local political choice that must be respected absent explicit constitutional language or history to the contrary, but downright immoral. The early indifference of public health agencies added the fillip that the punishment for sodomy could well be a death sentence. As Andriote put it, "choice" began to seem too frivolous a concept for their reality.

In *Lawrence v. Texas,* the ultimately successful 2003 challenge to the sodomy laws that overturned *Bowers,* a group of professors told the Supreme Court that "gay people usually appeared in the media in the 1950s only as shadowy and dangerous figures . . . but they now appear as a diverse and familiar group whose all-too-human struggles and pleasures draw the interest of large viewing audiences. It is not only in the media that heterosexuals see homosexuals. The growing openness of lesbians and gay men about their sexual orientation since the 1970s has had a tremendous impact on their relatives, friends, neighbors, and co-workers. Growing numbers of heterosexuals realize that some of the people they most love and respect are gay."

The movement for same-sex marriage is a direct outgrowth of that transformation. As a lead lawyer in the marriage movement, Evan Wolfson, put it, in a 2005 interview in *Mother Jones,* "We're fighting for the same freedom to marry that other Americans have and treasure—with the same rules, the same responsibilities, commitment, and the same respect." Although many commentators make the case for including gays by denigrating the spiritual and social seriousness of marriage as it has evolved, especially since the sexual revolution of the mid-1960s, Wolfson will have none of it. He describes the litigants as "qualified, committed couples who have made a personal commitment to one another who are doing the hard work of marriage already—who are caring for one another, raising kids, caring about their aging parents, paying taxes."

The strategic lesson for feminists is that values trump choice every time. When lesbian and gay activists began demanding respect for their full human lives, slowly, slowly the culture began to change.

The substantive lesson for feminists is that women, too, are entitled to full human lives. Women, who, right and left contend, can flourish fully in an entirely private context, need to show how a flourishing life includes the public virtues of work. Gay and lesbian people whose private lives were denied to them had to show the society how a flourishing life included the virtues of love. This is not the place for a full history of the lesbian and gay movement, but it is worthy of note that when feminists speak of full human lives for women instead of embracing "choice," the people, like David Brooks, who resist them, are reduced to making lousy naturalistic arguments about the family.

Dig a little into the Web site of the Institute for American Values, which found my case for feminist lives "judgmental," and you will find that in addition to the (nonjudgmental) mission of defending the family as the natural foundation of American society, the institute also publishes writings that define the family as the "natural" coming together of people for reproductive purposes. Not surprisingly, lesbians and gays correctly find these naturalistic and theocratic versions of domesticity very frightening. The movement's refusal to have personhood reduced to such material terms is crucial to its success so far, and the move to moral personhood (movement analyst E. J. Graff calls it "simple humanity") teaches a lesson feminism ignores to its peril.

A CALL FOR VALUES FEMINISM

The feminist movement has good values. It started with the clear description of a flourishing life in *The Feminine Mystique*. It has never lost sight of the deep commitment that women should have equal access to the goods of life that men have and that any good life requires a substantial dose of freedom in order to pursue that life.

When it has programs, the feminist movement has good programs. Protecting women who need abortions, who, statistics show, are mostly the poorest and most helpless women of all. The never-ending quest for day care, which is a safety net for working- and middle-class women, who are so exposed to the risks of childbearing. I was never much for the girls just wanna have fun bunch, but even Maureen Dowd says she's figured out that feminism was about more than your Manolos.

The problem is today's feminist agenda is just that—a bunch of programs unmoored from the values that started them in the first place. And so they fail. A million words have been written about how morality talk is rapidly pushing the "choice" strategy of the abortion rights movement into the dustbin of history. Why would anyone take feminism's call for day care seriously when feminism embraces the women who blog on about its dire effects? If women who believe that you should give up everything but the food in your mouth to stay home are feminists, why is feminism bothering with the fact that women aren't paid fairly in the workplace? If feminism supports the decision to choose yourself into dependency, where is the muscle for women's mastery over their own reproductive fates? Only when feminism returns to its roots in the value of a flourishing life for women will it get the traction to make any difference again. It will be a smaller movement, but if we've learned anything from the lesbian and gay movement, it's that you don't have to be everyone to be someone.

Organized feminism should say: We think adult women deserve to work as well as love. We think the educated middle-class women who were always the core of the feminist movement should seek and keep the interesting, well-paid jobs that middle-class men have. We think they should not marry and

have babies unless they have a clear bargain with the men in-
volved that the men will pull half the weight of the household
all the time. We think there should be job fairs for female college freshmen. The person who says the kindergarten teacher
can tell the difference between the abused children of working
mothers and the pampered darlings of the stay-at-home moms
is not a feminist. She is a shill for the religious right. Here's
the door.

We don't have a bunch of programs. We support *abortions*
because it is immoral to abandon the poor black and Hispanic
women who are the real victims of the sanctimonious "life"
crowd. Beyond that, if the women's movement wanted to make
a difference in the lives of women, it would focus on *one issue*
that it could win and which could form a base for a whole new
movement. That issue is the incredibly sexy subject of . . . taxes.

More women work than don't. More women vote than
don't. Married workingwomen pay a terrible penalty for their
ambition in the form of much higher taxes than single workers pay. And you'll have a broadly based coalition that cuts
across political, economic, and class lines, because it's all the
fault of the institution everybody loves to hate: the IRS.

Tell a married mother to get a job and you're a Nazi. Set up
a coercive government program that forces every ambitious career woman into paying a huge penalty in taxes for her uppity
ambition and you're a . . . U.S. congressman. There is something appealing about getting help simply by pulling the lever
in a polling booth rather than reenacting an Edward Albee
play every time the dishwasher needs emptying. With a fo-

cused, middle-class appeal to the people who vote in the greatest numbers feminism could focus on electing a Congress that would stop the IRS from chaining women to the stove.

The problem is both political parties, like liberals and conservatives, are guilty of the same failing: They actually think women belong at home. Otherwise, they would have changed the tax code long ago. The Democrats controlled Congress for most of the last half of the twentieth century. During that time, the only white voters reliably Democratic anymore were workingwomen, and the tax code hurts workingwomen. Why didn't the Democrats change the tax code? The Republicans were supposed to be the party of the balanced budget, and the tax code motivates women to work in the invisible, untaxed economy of the home, thus reducing the revenue the government takes in. Why didn't the Republicans change the tax code? And still the tax law forces women home. It's Time for Them to Go.

I cannot take credit for this part of the rules. A tax professor at the University of Southern California, Edward McCaffery, laid out the whole sorry story in a book, *Taxing Women*. As McCaffery relates it, in 1948, the Congress wanted to reward the returning veterans of the greatest generation by kicking the females of the greatest generation out of the jobs the women had taken while the men were away at war. They changed the tax code to institute, for the first time since 1913 when the tax system was created, "joint filing." Under joint filing, married couples add their incomes together. Here's a simplified example. If they were filing singly, she would not pay 40 percent of her salary in taxes; at $50,000, her average rate would be more like 25 percent. But his $100,000 salary quickly climbs the ladder of the graduated income tax system, and the last few dollars he brings in are taxed at the highest, marginal, rate. And so is her entire salary. So when the moment comes for them to decide if she should quit and stay home with the baby, they are treating her salary of $50,000 as a take home of $30,000, instead of, say, her single take home of $37,500. If they had not married, they would be paying tens of thousands of dollars fewer in taxes. It is irresistible. Joint marital filing hurts the lesser earner. And until women start paying heed to the first set of rules and finding the money, the lesser earner might as well be wearing a frilly apron.

Every time a couple sharpens its pencils to decide what to do about child care when the second baby comes, the tax man is in the room. In 1997, McCaffery recommended that the United States "should consider moving to a system of separate filing . . . and look into and eliminate lower-income marriage penalties." He predicted what would happen regarding his suggestions: nothing. "Nothing is always the easiest thing to do. Conservatives always have this advantage, this final trump. Contemporary cognitive psychology teaches us that we all think in ways that are deeply wedded to the way things are. . . . We don't like change and we especially don't like losses." And nothing has been done.

It's simple, it's clean, it does not encourage women to stay home, as other prescriptions like paid housework do, and it doesn't involve the completely irrational arguments about day care and the well-being of women. Right now the television is full of the Ms. Foundation's quadrennial fantasy, "Someday a

Woman Will Be President." Closest we've come is the actress Geena Davis. I'd settle for a little more in my take-home pay every week any day.

SOMETIMES IT *IS* BRAIN SURGERY

I got a letter from a doctor. He thought my article was crap. His wife was leading the moral life, he claimed, and only his weak character made him so greedy he went on practicing medicine rather than spending more time with their children. I figured he was doing face-lifts or something. I wrote him back asking him to tell me more. As he described his and his wife's deal, it sounded pretty good. She's a highly educated physician who works half time at a family practice, which enables her to spend time with their children and do most of the errands and housework as well as volunteering at the local soup kitchen. He practices medicine full time. Only when I pressed him on why he worked such long hours and neglected his children, by his lights, did it emerge what he is doing. He's doing research on children's cancer. So there it is. He probably won't, but he just may, find a cure for cancer. And she never will.

ACKNOWLEDGMENTS

It's never easy playing Cassandra. The Trojans thought the horse was just adorable, and Agammemnon thought he'd get a hero's welcome home. I am all the more grateful, therefore, for the people who supported this project in the earliest times, when it seemed no one would ever listen.

Thanks to professional friends: my agent, Neeti Madan, of Sterling Lord Literistic, who said it was the story she saw everywhere she looked and would not let it die; to Esther Kartiganer, late of *60 Minutes,* who thought the point of view should be heard and to the good people at *60 Minutes* who agreed, Lesley Stahl, Shari Finkelstein, and Sianne Garlick; and to Carol Felsenthal, who jump-started my writing career so many years ago. No one is more entitled to gratitude than the people at *The American Prospect,* particularly the supportive and resourceful editor in chief, Michael Tomasky, who took on the liberal orthodoxy, and to my editor at Viking Penguin, wonderful Wendy Wolf, who knows what she wants and never loses her sense of humor, and to the designer, Nancy Resnick, and all the other hardworking people in the Viking managing editorial, production, and design departments who, when things got tight, just rolled up their sleeves and went . . . to work. To my indefatigable research assistant, Michelle Saint.

Above all, credit is due to *American Prospect* Deputy Editor Sarah Blustain. From the moment she called last summer until yesterday, she saw the truth in the story. She was fearless in advancing its public airing against formidable odds, and she is an editor so gifted she could make

Bulwer-Lytton read like Jane Austen. Finally, like E. B. White's Charlotte, she is "a true friend and a good writer."

A paragraph of her own for author and neighbor Sheila Buff, who flogged me out of the garden with the injunction to keep pitching last July. You are an angel and we are so grateful to have you to share good times and bad.

Thanks to the civilian friends and family: my optimistic, supportive, loving, resourceful husband (happily married for seventeen years, bloggers, take that!), who listened to me prophesy without result for four long years. To our daughters, examples all. To my best friend of fifty years, Connie Abrams, and her partner, Ann Verber, a lifelong support system, Connie editing a thousand versions. To Dan Farrell Davis, who saw a great future for me. To the women of Brandeis University's Women's Studies Program and Center and particularly to Helaine Allen and Cynthia Berenson, and to E. J. Graff and Stephanie Coontz for their advice. To everyone who listened to me at dinner parties, east and west, and reminded me in the darkest times that I had seen something that needed to be described.

To the media men of the right, who know a worthy adversary when they see one—Bernard Goldberg, who took an obscure academic and made her famous by naming her to his One Hundred Screwups list, and to David Brooks, who took a policy article and turned it into a national cause célèbre in order to show how wrong it was. We shall see.

SOURCES

FACTS

The 1996 and 2005 *New York Times* Sunday "Styles" section gave me my brides (and grooms).

The U.S. government gave me everyone else:
- "America's Families and Living Arrangements: 2003," U.S. Census Bureau, November 2004.
- "Fertility of American Women: June 2004," U.S. Census Bureau, December 2005.
- "Women in the Labor Force: A Databook," U.S. Department of Labor, Bureau of Labor Statistics, May 2005.
- "Fertility of American Women: June 2002," U.S. Census Bureau, October 2003.
- "'Stay-at-Home' Parents Top 5 Million, Census Bureau Reports," U.S. Census Bureau, news release, November 30, 2004.
- "Issues in Labor Statistics, Are Managers and Professionals Really Working More?" U.S. Department of Labor, Bureau of Labor Statistics, May 2000.

I used lots of great studies of women:
- "Data Quality of Housework Hours in the Panel Study of Income Dynamics: Who Really Does the Dishes?," Alexandra C. Achen and Frank P. Stafford, Institute for Social Research, University of Michigan, September 2005.

- "Men Do More Housework Than Women Think," Sue Shellenbarger, *Wall Street Journal Online,* May 20, 2005.
- "Participation in Education," U.S. Department of Education, National Center for Education Statistics, 2005.
- "Off-Ramps and On-Ramps: Keeping Talented Women on the Road to Success," Ann Sylvia Hewlett, Carolyn Buck Luce, Harvard Business Publishing, March 1, 2005.
- "Diversity and Demographics: A Current Glance of Women in the Law 2003," American Bar Association, 2003.
- "Women in the Fortune 500," Catalyst Organization, 2005.
- "Women in State Policy Leadership 1998–2005," Center for Women in Government and Civil Society, University at Albany, 2006.
- "Women in the Media," Martha M. Lauzen, School of Communication, San Diego State University, 2004.
- "Disparate Burden," Scott Jaschik, www.InsideHigher Ed.com, 2005.
- "Marriage and Baby Blues: Re-defining Gender Equity," Mary Ann Mason and Marc Goulden, paper delivered October 30, 2003 at Mommies and Daddies on the Fast Track: Success of Parents in Demanding Profession conference at University of Pennsylvania.
- "Gender Differences in Pay," Francine D. Blau and Lawrence M. Kahn, National Bureau of Economic Research, Inc., 2000.
- "Are Women Opting Out? Debunking the Myth," Heather Boushey, Center for Economic and Policy Research, 2005.
- "Induced Abortion in the United States," The Guttmacher Institute, 2005.

OPINION

The world of opinion has been transformed by the rise of the blogosphere. From Nobel Prize-winning intellectuals like Gary Becker, www.becker-posner-blog.com, to what seems like every stay-at-home mom in America. If there are six million SAHMs, there are probably an equal number

of blogs. I often followed the debate on www.bloggingbaby.com, www.
urbanbaby.com, www.literarymama.com, and www.mothersmovement.
org. Mothersmovement.org was a good source for what passes for feminist activism on the family at present, carried the interview with Miriam
Peskowitz, author of *Beyond the Mommy Wars,* and had a particularly use-
ful compendium of the attacks, "Everybody Hates Linda." Everyone's a
critic as they say. Bloggingbaby.com unwittingly did a lot of research for
me when they asked women to tell their stories.

The wonderful description of managing your husband's housekeeping comes from the Blog Bitch PhD: http://bitchphd.blogspot.com/
2006/02/forecast-frigidity-in-south-dakota.html.

On February 22, the Christian Web site WorldViews carried an anec-
dote that reproduced verbatim what one of the guests on *Good Morning
America* had put forth as her own personal experience. Here it is:

> A kindergarten teacher once commented, "I can tell almost as
> soon as they come into the classroom [sic], the difference between
> the two types of children."
>
> My friend asked, "If they come from Christian homes or non-
> Christian homes?"
>
> The teacher: "No. Whether or not they had stay-at-home
> mothers." She went on to explain that the children who were
> raised at home were more secure, more confident, and more ready
> to learn.

http://www.worldmagblog.com/blog/archives/022806.html

Danielle Crittenden shared her opinion of workingwomen ("pile of pay
stubs") on Boundless Webzine, www.boundless.org/2005/articles.

The guys blog a lot, too. I heard from them at http://www.
joannejacobs.com/mtarchives/015759.html, www.crosswalk.com/news/
weblogs/mohler, and http://atbozzo.blogspot.com/2005/12/eighty-hour-

work-week-no-thank-you.html, especially about how much they hate work (http://11d.typepad.com/blog/2005/11/we_hate_mommies.html.)

The Chicago Women's Liberation Union Web site was invaluable for women's history, http://www.cwluherstory.com/CWLUArchive/polhousework.html, and was the source of Pat Mainardi's wonderful essay, originally published by the Redstockings, on housework. The Mark Twain quote is actually, "The man who does not read books has no advantage over the man that cannot read them." Home.san.it.com/keestone/quotes.html.

Oregon has a very informative Web site about the assisted-suicide law, jttp//Oregon.gov.DHS.

The conservative Institute for American Values runs a "family scholars" Web site, http://familyscholars.org.

Plato's *Republic* is available free, online at http://classics.mit.edu/Plato/republic.html.

The suggestion that employers not hire women comes from Marty Nemko, Conservative Battleline Online, October 6, 2004.

The eighty-hour week has a lively Web presence, atbozzo, above, and http://phantomscribbler.blogspot.com/2005/12/another-willing-tool-of-patriarchy-has.html.

The *New York Times* provided unlimited coverage of the so-called Opt-Out Revolution, starting with Lisa Belkin, "The Opt-Out Revolution," *New York Times Magazine,* October 26, 2003, followed by Louise Story, "Many Women at Elite Colleges Set Career Path to Motherhood," September 20, 2005, justified ex ante on the Web edition only, "Background: Reporting on the Aspirations of Young Women," by Louise Story; and my personal favorite, Tina Kelley, "Toilet Training at 6 Months? Better Take a Seat," *New York Times,* October 9, 2005.

It was David Brooks's *Boboes in Paradise* that first alerted me to the *New York Times* wedding announcements as a distant early warning system for social change. Brooks's column about my article, "The Year of

Domesticity," appeared on January 1, 2006, in the op-ed pages of the *New York Times* alongside the cautionary tale "Modern Love, Paradise Lost" by Terry Martin Hekker, January 1, 2006.

I learned a lot from the reactions to my work in the mainstream media, including Suzanne Goldenberg's "In the World of Self-Imposed Mental Enslavement," *Guardian,* January 14, 2006, on how alien women find the concept of marital bargaining; Salon.com's Rebecca Traister's "At Home with David Brooks," January 1, 2006; Patricia Cohen's "The Nation: Today, Some Feminists Hate the Word 'Choice,'" *New York Times,* January 15, 2006; Judith Warner's "The Parent Trap," *New York Times,* op-ed page, February 8, 2006.

And finally, I got letters (to the editor of *The American Prospect*) about how women's choices are all hormone driven, how public school was not for *their* family, and how they spend the time singing and climbing trees since they graduated from Harvard.

THEORY AND HISTORY

Andriote, Michael. *Victory Deferred.* Chicago: University of Chicago Press, 1999.

Becker, Gary. *A Treatise on the Family.* Cambridge, MA: Harvard University Press, 1981, and articles preceding it.

Buller, David. *Adapting Minds: Evolutionary Psychology and the Persistent Quest for Human Nature.* Boston: Bradford Books, MIT Press, 2005.

Chethik, Neil. *VoiceMale—What Husbands Really Think About Their Marriages, Their Wives, Sex, Housework, and Commitment.* New York: Simon & Schuster, 2006.

Coontz, Stephanie. *Marriage: A History.* New York: Viking, 2005.

Cosmides, Leda and John Tooby. *Evolutionary Psychology: A Primer.* Santa Barbara: Center for Evolutionary Psychology, University of California at Santa Barbara, 1997.

Ephron, Nora. *Heartburn.* New York: Vintage Contemporary, 1996.

Fein, Ellen and Sherrie Schneider. *The Rules: Time-Tested Secrets for Capturing the Heart of Mr. Right.* New York: Warner Books, 1996.

Friedan, Betty. *The Feminine Mystique.* New York: Dell Publishing, 1964 (ancient yellowing copy from college).

———. *The Second Stage.* New York: Summit Books, 1981.

Gilligan, Carol. *In a Different Voice: Psychology and Women's Moral Development.* Cambridge, MA: Harvard University Press, 1993.

Grossbard-Shectman, Shoshana A., ed. *Marriage and the Economy: Theory and Evidence from Advanced Industrial Societies.* Cambridge, Eng.: Cambridge University Press, 2003.

Hennessee, Judith. *Betty Friedan: Her Life.* New York: Random House, 2005.

McCaffery, Edward J. *Taxing Women.* Chicago: University of Chicago Press, 1997.

Mahoney, Rhona. *Kidding Ourselves: Babies, Breadwinning and Bargaining Power.* New York: Basic Books, 1995. Nothing in my book would have been possible without the groundbreaking work of this book.

Moen, Phyllis and Patricia Roehling. *The Career Mystique: Cracks in the American Dream.* Lanham, MD: Rowman and Littlefield, 2005.

Pollak, Robert A. "Bargaining Power in Marriage: Earnings, Wage Rates and Household Production," paper delivered at Washington University in St. Louis, March 2005.

Santorum, Richard. *It Takes a Family: Conservatism and the Common Good.* Wilmington, DE: Intercollegiate Studies Institute, July 4, 2005.

Stern, Sydney Ladensohn. *Gloria Steinem: Her Passions, Politics, and Mystique.* New York: Birch Lane Press, 1997.

Warner, Judith. *Perfect Madness: Motherhood in an Age of Anxiety.* New York: Riverhead 2005.

Williams, Joan. *Unbending Gender: Why Family and Work Conflict and What to Do About It.* Oxford, Eng.: Oxford University Press, 2001. I'm deeply indebted to her for the Deborah Fallows story and analysis.

In addition to the many books on theory and history, there were also wonderful essays on Salon.com and in the *New York Times Book Review* on the lives of Betty Friedan and Gloria Steinem and the early feminist movement: Laura Miller, "When Feminists Were Divas," in Salon and "Outside Agitator," by Judith Shulevitz, *New York Times,* May 9, 1999; good work on the antifeminist Phyllis Schlafly at http://www.legacy98.org/move-hist.html and in a tribute, "Conservatives' First Lady Sparked Pro-Family Effort," Ralph Z. Hallow, *Washington Times,* October 7, 2005; and on gay marriage, "The Battle to Say 'I Do,'" Michael Beckel, *Mother Jones,* October 10, 2005.

FOR THE BEST IN PAPERBACKS, LOOK FOR THE

In every corner of the world, on every subject under the sun, Penguin represents quality and variety—the very best in publishing today.

For complete information about books available from Penguin—including Penguin Classics and Puffins—and how to order them, write to us at the appropriate address below. Please note that for copyright reasons the selection of books varies from country to country.

In the United States: Please write to *Penguin Group (USA), P.O. Box 12289 Dept. B, Newark, New Jersey 07101-5289* or call *1-800-788-6262*.

In the United Kingdom: Please write to *Dept. EP, Penguin Books Ltd, Bath Road, Harmondsworth, West Drayton, Middlesex UB7 0DA*.

In Canada: Please write to *Penguin Books Canada Ltd, 90 Eglinton Avenue East, Suite 700, Toronto, Ontario M4P 2Y3*.

In Australia: Please write to *Penguin Books Australia Ltd, P.O. Box 257, Ringwood, Victoria 3134*.

In New Zealand: Please write to *Penguin Books (NZ) Ltd, Private Bag 102902, North Shore Mail Centre, Auckland 10*.

In India: Please write to *Penguin Books India Pvt Ltd, 11 Panchsheel Shopping Centre, Panchsheel Park, New Delhi 110 017*.

In the Netherlands: Please write to *Penguin Books Netherlands bv, Postbus 3507, NL-1001 AH Amsterdam*.

In Germany: Please write to *Penguin Books Deutschland GmbH, Metzlerstrasse 26, 60594 Frankfurt am Main*.

In Spain: Please write to *Penguin Books S. A., Bravo Murillo 19, 1° B, 28015 Madrid*.

In Italy: Please write to *Penguin Italia s.r.l., Via Benedetto Croce 2, 20094 Corsico, Milano*.

In France: Please write to *Penguin France, Le Carré Wilson, 62 rue Benjamin Baillaud, 31500 Toulouse*.

In Japan: Please write to *Penguin Books Japan Ltd, Kaneko Building, 2-3-25 Koraku, Bunkyo-Ku, Tokyo 112*.

In South Africa: Please write to *Penguin Books South Africa (Pty) Ltd, Private Bag X14, Parkview, 2122 Johannesburg*.